Half-Light

Half-Light

WESTBOUND ON A HOT PLANET

AMY KALER

UNIVERSITY *of* **ALBERTA** PRESS

Published by

University of Alberta Press
1–16 Rutherford Library South
11204 89 Avenue NW
Edmonton, Alberta, Canada T6G 2J4
amiskwaciwâskahikan | Treaty 6 |
Métis Territory
ualbertapress.ca | uapress@ualberta.ca

LIBRARY AND ARCHIVES CANADA
CATALOGUING IN PUBLICATION

Title: Half-light : westbound on a hot planet
    / Amy Kaler.
Names: Kaler, Amy, author.
Series: Wayfarer (Edmonton, Alta.)
Description: Series statement: Wayfarer |
    Includes bibliographical references.
Identifiers: Canadiana (print) 20230553877 |
    Canadiana (ebook) 20230553990 |
    ISBN 9781772127409 (softcover) |
    ISBN 9781772127607 (EPUB) |
    ISBN 9781772127614 (PDF)
Subjects: LCSH: Kaler, Amy—Travel—North
    America. | LCSH: North America—
    Description and travel. | LCSH: Climatic
    changes. | LCSH: Travel—Psychological
    aspects. | LCGFT: Travel writing.
Classification: LCC E41 .K35 2024 |
    DDC 917.04/542—dc23

First edition, first printing, 2024.
First printed and bound in Canada by
Houghton Boston Printers, Saskatoon,
Saskatchewan.
Copyediting and proofreading by
Mary Lou Roy.

University of Alberta Press is committed to
protecting our natural environment. As part
of our efforts, this book is printed on Enviro
Paper: it contains 100% post-consumer
recycled fibres and is acid- and chlorine-free.

University of Alberta Press gratefully
acknowledges the support received for its
publishing program from the Government
of Canada, the Canada Council for the Arts,
and the Government of Alberta through the
Alberta Media Fund.

In loving memory of
John Otis Kaler, 1932–2020
Hilary Kay Kaler (Spooner), 1935–2022

"How will you go about finding that thing the nature of which is totally unknown to you?"…[is] the basic tactical question in life. The things we want are transformative, and we don't know or only think we know what is on the other side of that transformation. Love, wisdom, grace, inspiration— how do you go about finding these things that are in some ways about extending the boundaries of the self into unknown territory, about becoming someone else?

    —REBECCA SOLNIT, *A Field Guide to Getting Lost*

Thou shouldst not have been old till thou hadst been wise.

    —WILLIAM SHAKESPEARE, *King Lear*

Don't let me hear you say life's taking you nowhere.

    —DAVID BOWIE, "Golden Years"

Contents

Prologue

THIS BOOK IS ABOUT THREE THINGS: getting older in a mortal body; living during a climate catastrophe; and the North American settler west, centred on my home city of Edmonton in the province of Alberta. In other words, it's about getting older during an environmental catastrophe in western Canada. It is not authoritative on any of those counts. I do not have any wisdom to impart about how to age gracefully or productively; I cannot comprehend, much less resolve, the collapse of the dynamic systems that produce Earth's climate; and I am not trying to write a history of the settler west in Canada.

What I can do is tell you how these things—age, climate, west—braid together in my life, and what it is like to be aware of them all at once. My perspective is that of a woman of white settler descent in her mid-fifties, living and still settling in a mid-sized city in northwestern Canada, over the span of a couple of years that have encompassed the hottest, coldest, wettest, and driest days ever recorded in this place.

I am never unaware of the mess that humans have made, and often take refuge in the more-than-human world—snow goose migrations, golden tamarack stands, pulses of the river—and I write about that too. These are the beings that were here before humans arrived in the west, they have lived beside us, and some of them, at least, will still be here whenever humans depart.

And because I am human myself and therefore kin to the people who have made and unmade the west, I am fascinated by what was left behind by the making and unmaking. I am drawn to the ruined and

< *Abandoned farmhouse on the Alberta prairie.* (Photo by Michel Figeat.)

abandoned, the places in the west that are no longer what they used to be, or that will never be what they might once have been. In these pages, I take you to an abandoned Cold War–era observatory in a hamlet in central Alberta, a field of old cars in the badlands, a civil defence bunker in Edmonton, and an empty Orthodox church on the prairie, among many other places. I tell you what these places look like, and share the stories that I've learned about them.

I alternate my accounts of places that I've visited with short reflections that explore the inner world of someone who knows both that she is getting older and that her planet is in trouble. This means attending to mortal thoughts, as my own finitude becomes more and more clear to me, as the light starts to fade. It also means trying to be an honest witness to the disintegration of the world that I knew, my world, which is now in the grip of climate change.

What follows, then, is a series of notes on westboundedness, in three senses—the place called the west, as I live in it and through it; the inevitability of aging and moving towards the sunset years; and the knowledge that the entire planet is tipping towards the blazing sun in the western sky, or perhaps that the sun itself is setting, tipping us into half-light.

Westbound names all these things. I am bound to the west in ways that I am only now beginning to explore—geographically, temporally, and metaphorically. The western horizon, the place of the setting sun, the dimming day, is where I am going as I move into the last few decades of my life, and of the life of a world that seems to be heating up and falling apart.

Central Alberta, Somewhere Near Rumsey

ON THE ROAD TO DRUMHELLER. Early summer, when the flowers have sprung but before they dry up. Smell of sage on the air, spicy and calming at once. Picked handfuls of sage at Dry Island Buffalo Jump, up on the escarpment that overlooks the distant Red Deer River. The striations in the cliffs across the valley include the ashes thrown up by an asteroid strike that blasted a hole in the Gulf of Mexico sixty-six million years ago, turned the sky black, and ended the age of dinosaurs.

Today I have the freedom of going where I want, taking random backroads and long ways around. Endless undulating rangeland, splashes of yellow. Small railroad towns in the aspen parkland, at their prettiest, bright sun in the clear sky and the elms all lush and green. The medians down the wide main boulevards of towns like Bashaw are a shadow of an old idea of gentility. Every town has a Railway Avenue. Most have a few empty storefronts. Here and there, a collapsed farmhouse.

There's supposed to be an old school building around here, called Stonepile. First it was a school, then it was the office of the United

< Rolling landscape of grassland and woodland near Rumsey, Alberta.
(Photo by the author.)

1

Farmers of Alberta, then it was a Masonic lodge, then it was a church, and then it was closed. The stone pile of the name may have been a cairn—created by Indigenous inhabitants, found by settlers, used by both to distinguish one place in the valley from another. I haven't seen the building with my own eyes; I've just heard about it. It's down one of those gravel roads or single-tracks that I didn't take, not this time.

Spectacular descents into the Red Deer River valley where the flat-land suddenly falls away. Cottonwood, larch, silverberry, mugwort, wild rose.

This part of Alberta is the heart of the settler west, used as the backdrop for that genre of books and movies known as westerns, redolent of creosote and tumbleweed. Ghost towns or near-ghost-towns like Dorothy and Wayne have been used by budget-conscious directors as settings for everything from *Superman* to *Brokeback Mountain* to music videos by Tom Jones and Tom Cochrane, because they're cheaper than the Montana or Wyoming alternatives. Western myth-making has thrived here, even as much of the rest of the local economy has bounced up and down, reverberating with the price of oil and coal.

This mythical settler west takes many forms. It's the cowboy west, the last best west, the frontier, the endless forest, the flat prairie, the agrarian lands, the oil and coal of the ancient seabed under the ground. The railroad that connected it all. The little towns strung like pearls on an iron strand laid across the prairie and through the mountains. The distances between the towns. The farms that failed, the farms that grew and grew until canola and winter wheat fields splayed out to the horizon. And the mid-century modern west—the sunset over the sprawling ranch-style house in the suburbs of Calgary or Edmonton, the space race, the affluence and technological optimism built on the promise that there would always be more. The dream of the frontier extending into space, into the sky. Even today, when I'm travelling around Alberta, I see the fluttering outlines of these myths, some of which cleave closely to things that really happened and some of which are entirely made up.

After a couple of decades in Alberta, I'm canny enough not to buy into the illusions of the frontier and the Indigenous erasures on which they're predicated, but I'm also steeped enough in those illusions, cinematic and literary, that something resonates within me when I see the land dropping straight down to the old watercourses, brown and silver and green of willows. The West. That's where I'm going, that's where I am.

Westbound

I NEVER INTENDED TO BE A WESTERNER, yet here I am. I've been in Alberta since the start of the twenty-first century. I'm bound to this place by those decades, not by conscious choice or by inheritance. I am not a westerner by birth and ancestry, unlike the Indigenous peoples or the latecoming white settlers of the nineteenth and twentieth centuries, although I am inhabiting the places they made. I do not belong here in a deep sense.

But If I don't belong here, I don't belong anywhere else either. I'm here because of a contingency of the labour market at the beginning of the millennium—I was offered a tenure-track academic job in Edmonton in 2000. For me and hundreds of thousands of people looking for work back then, North America was tipped up like an unsteady folding table and we rolled down the incline into the west. We were westbound by necessity. We did not begin as westerners.

But over the decades, I've become a westerner by transpiration. I've settled into this place by breathing in the mixture of sage and sky and settler towns laid out like wire fencing on the gold and beige of the prairie—and also by inhaling the knowledge of how the white latecomers tried to eradicate the earlier people, and the knowledge that this is still treaty land. The air of this place is failure and ruin, as well as beauty.

And while I am geographically westbound, in a place whose past is not mine, or at least not mine by choice, I am also bound *for* the west in a chronological and mythical sense, no matter where I may be in space. I began connecting these ideas around the time I realized that

I was more than halfway into the journey known as "going west," a euphemism for the end of life, following the sun as it crosses the sky and sinks into the horizon.

My fifty-fifth birthday is now behind me, so I can no longer claim to be in my early fifties. I got my first senior discounts without even asking, thanks to grey hair. Among my age-peers, the people I have known since I was a child, some are retiring or having grandchildren or starting to die, and not dying from the freak accidents that take out young and healthy people but from the sorts of conditions that take decades to accrete. The finish line is coming into view.

I'm not in the midst of life transitions. I underwent a time of upheaval in the early 2010s—a quarter-century marriage that ended in divorce and then death, a move to a new home, a transition to full-time single parenting, a new relationship, a couple of significant professional promotions. These things happened in the middle of my life, but I didn't think of myself as middle-aged until very recently. My awareness of my own age stalled at some point, and if I didn't know the year of my birth, I'd consider myself someone in her early forties, equal parts of life behind and before.

But that is not the truth, and I'm starting to see that the road ahead of me is shorter than the road I've travelled. It's increasingly likely that everything I've done in my life so far is everything that I will do. Simultaneously, the list of things that I will not do in my life is getting longer, and one of those things is moving out of Alberta, getting out of the west. I'm probably westbound from now until the end.

The idea of the west as the end, as the direction towards which human life tends, is broadly shared across cultures. The ancient Egyptians imagined the sun god Ra travelling westward through the sky each day, to "die" in the underworld of Duat. He rode two boats in this journey—the morning boat that took him from dawn to midday was called Matet, or "becoming strong"; the evening boat taking him from noon to sunset was Semktet, or "becoming weak."

Among the Celtic inhabitants of the British Isles, from whom I am descended, the west is the direction of endings, of mysteries and formlessness, perhaps suggested by the unknowns that lay beyond the western horizon of the North Atlantic. A fragment of a thirteenth-century Gaelic poem laments that wind, water, women, and men all inevitably go west. Hundreds of years later, Alfred Lord Tennyson, put the west and death into the mouth of his poetic version of Ulysses, whose purpose is "to sail beyond the sunset and the paths / of the western stars, until I die."

The Chinese Buddhist tradition includes the Pure Land of the West, at the far end of the Golden Bridge, where the souls of the deceased go if they have been virtuous enough to merit an escape from the cycle of rebirth. In Meso-American religious traditions, those who died in child-birth followed Cihuacóatl, the goddess of fertility, to the sunset and beyond.

In public and private reporting during the First World War, "to go west" meant a death in battle, something that could not be mentioned directly in letters home so as not to shock the recipients. This may be connected to older British antecedents, in which "going west" referred to the last journey taken by condemned prisoners in London: from Newgate Prison to the gallows at what is now the Marble Arch.

Sometime during the last few years, I realized that I, too, was well and truly westbound. Westboundedness is a complex condition, and I may spend the rest of my life reckoning with it.

Retlaw

WE BLUNDERED INTO THE GHOST TOWN OF RETLAW, my partner and I, on an unearthly winter day, when the daytime surface temperature in Alberta was lower than that recorded by the Mars lander. These ultra-cold days have been more frequent over the last decade. Maybe the air has changed as weather becomes more extreme, or maybe my senses have only now tuned in to the absolute clarity of the icy atmosphere, the shift that occurs when cold is no longer a property of the air but is simply the air itself.

Retlaw was at the heart of the puzzle-grids that divide up this stretch of southern Alberta, between Enchant and Rolling Hills. We'd found it in an online list of Alberta ghost towns and set out that morning, coming out of Medicine Hat in a series of right-angle turns, as the roads got rougher, the land flatter, and the passing vehicles fewer. We passed field after field of stubble buried almost entirely under snow, silent since the end of the grain harvest a few months back. Then we passed the elevation of a new kind of field, in the form of rows of solar panels marching off to the horizon. Solar farms are still so new and odd and perhaps controversial in this part of the province that the entire array was surrounded by high wire fences topped with tiny cameras. The grain crops had fences that would only keep out low-slung animals and differentiate one farmer's land from another's; the fences around the solar panels are proprietary and defensive.

From the range road that runs alongside Retlaw, almost nothing can be seen of the former town except a square white United Church

< *Remnants of domestic life in Retlaw, Alberta.* (Photo by the author.)

building with the characteristic corner bell tower. The land undulates slightly where the town used to be, its curves accented by the drifts of snow. As we pulled in to where our maps said we should find Retlaw's numbered streets, we saw a single still-occupied house. A sociable farm dog came running out to meet us, bounding through the snow, overcome with the excitement of visitors. The dog and house must have had an owner, but we saw no human inhabitants.

We braced against the stunning cold to get out of the car and pace, looking for Retlaw's remains. At first there was nothing at all to see, and then slowly the outlines of the town started to assemble themselves, out of snowdrifts and collapsed walls and scattered handwritten signs about the glory days a hundred years ago.

Even when this place was booming, it was a brief candle. In 1913, there was just a post office called Barney on the site; then there was a railway spur and a station called Retlaw ("Walter" spelled backwards, after CPR official Walter Baker); then there was a town with two restaurants, a hotel, an opera house, four grain elevators, and a police station; then the dry years got worse; then the Bow River Irrigation District built a crucial irrigation canal fifteen kilometres to the east of Retlaw, near the town of Vauxhall; then everyone started to move out of Retlaw, and by 1925 almost all the people were gone. Retlaw has been the place where a town used to be for almost ten times as long as the town existed.

Doing the historical math leaves me with the dizzy feeling of trying to fit together time scales that are vastly larger, but still exist in ratios that are hard to grasp—for example, the time that humans have been on Earth in relation to the entire existence of the planet, or the size of the planet compared with the one-to-seventy-thousand scale model of Earth that I saw at the Muttart Conservatory back in Edmonton. Or, closer to home, the history of European settlers in the west set against the history of the Indigenous peoples: a century or two compared with tens of millennia.

Here in south-central Alberta, I'm in a part of the west that is indebted to the deepest of deep time. This land was once the Western Interior Seaway, or the Niobrara Sea, an enormous inland ocean that separated the east side of North America from the west. For millions of years, the warm salty waters of the seaway seethed with sharks, squid-like invertebrates, mollusks, bony fish, and marine reptiles, which swam, mated, died, and sank. Their remains and the remains of the plants they fed on became the coal, oil, and natural gas that we've been pulling out of the ground for the last eighty or so years, the fossil energy era less than a blink of time. The solar farm we passed may be the next blink, if we're lucky enough to be around for another century, drawing down energy from the sun rather than up from the ground.

Time contracts and expands. Consider the brief life of this town that "went ghost"; the few generations of Europeans inventing a thing called Alberta and putting their names on mountains and lakes and towns; the many more generations of Indigenous people who gave this place its oldest names; and the twentieth-century moment that I've spent most of my life in, of constant expansion and consumption, fuelled by the fossils, which is delivering us all inexorably to a long time of privation and contraction, assuming we manage to avoid outright destruction. It's a snarl of temporalities—pull on one moment of experience and something much larger unspools from the tangle of time past, present, and future.

Retlaw blinked in and out of existence. It disappeared as a living town—the only building that still functions is the United Church—but embarked on a long half-life as a memory. This memory is not just housed in official records of land acquisition and division. The site is speckled with handwritten, very unofficial signs announcing what structure was on which exact spot a hundred years ago, what people would have lived or worked in the building, or passed through it, and what happened to them. There's no indication of the author's name. Someone keeps this memory alive—not just the knowledge that Retlaw existed, but the specifics of who, when, where, and why. There is still work going on here, the work of remembering and reminding.

We learn, for instance, that E.K. Parks moved to Retlaw in 1925, just as the town was sliding down the far side of prosperity. His son Manny ran a gas station near the Retlaw townsite until 1956. Manny passed away in 1985, at the age of eighty. The Retlaw Hotel opened in 1913 with thirty-two rooms connected by call bells, and served as a temporary school. The owner, Charles LaRosse, set aside several rooms to be used for a private hospital run by his wife, identified only as "Mrs LaRosse." Elmer Merriman came to Retlaw from New York state in 1913 and ran a stagecoach route between Retlaw and the town of Taber. He hauled mail, groceries, coal, and medicine, a trip of twenty-five miles that took two days. The same year that Elmer Merriman came to town, the Retlaw Opera House opened, managed by Clifford Beardsley. Local Methodists used the opera house for church services, and the sign on which this information is recorded states, rather cryptically, that "after the 13th of December, the hall could be rented for any social gatherings."

Near a small cenotaph, a grove of signs—sheets of laser-printed paper stapled to a wooden frame and covered by plastic—tells of the men of Retlaw who fought in the Second World War. Dick Foulkes was part of the 112th Light Anti-Aircraft Battery, which was made up of men from the surrounding area. Dick was in Germany, France, Belgium, and Holland, and was in England for D-Day. When the war was over, the signs tell us, "Dick wasn't one to stay in one place for too long, and worked as a ranch hand on several ranches in Alberta. Later he worked in feed lots and broke horses. He is now retired and enjoying life." John Bennett, a field surveyor with the RCAF, met a Scottish girl, Joan Parker, in London, where they married in 1944. The wedding ring and the wedding cake were both shipped over from Alberta. The Bennetts returned to Retlaw after the war to take over farming from John Bennett's widowed father, but the farm was plagued with grasshoppers and cutworms, and hail destroyed two of the first seven years' crops. The Bennetts sold the farm, left Retlaw, and moved to Calgary.

One half-collapsed building holds a scatter of household items— a sewing machine, a kettle, a boot, a table set on bricks. Pale-green crackled paint is peeling off the walls. According to the sign in front of it, this was the former post office and the real estate office of Elmer Merriman. Then the Yaroslawskys lived there, then the Waterfields. The last inhabitant was one Harold Price, who left in 1989. Visitors are warned not to enter. The division between the inside of the building and the outside is purely notional—doors are missing, walls are gaping, and the snow has sedimented itself onto the floors and other flat surfaces, like the ancient inhabitants of the Niobrara Sea, settling down to rest. The structure is a paradox, a bit of temporal collapse or tesseract. Someone might have been sitting on that chair or boiling that teakettle just a moment ago, possibly Harold Price or one of the Yaroslawskys, yet the piles of snow and broken wood speak of desolation.

Driving out of Retlaw that day, leaving early against the oncoming dusk, our car hit a patch of frozen ground concealed by a snowdrift and spun out. In the passenger seat I saw the world spin around one and a half times before the car juddered to a stop, buried in the roadside drift, pointing the way we'd come. My partner is an experienced winter driver, and he managed to corral the spin just enough that we were slowed, that our impact was gentle enough that the airbags didn't deploy, and that the car didn't roll over. This is how people die on the backroads in winter, so his skills may have saved us. The spinout took only a few seconds, but those were long seconds: long enough for me to think, *I don't want to have a visual memory of what's happening so I should close my eyes*, long enough to register that the snow seemed to be sucking the car in as we ground to a halt.

Luckily we could get cellphone reception; luckily I had an automobile association membership; luckily there was a tow truck that could get to us before dark; luckily we had half a tank of gas and could run the engine for warmth; luckily the tow truck was able to pull us out; luckily we made it to our destination—Drumheller—that night before the gas ran out completely.

Time contracts and expands. That hour and a half after the spinout, before the rescue by the tow truck, seemed to elongate into an era of its own. In a small metal box on the winter prairie, half-swallowed by the snow, time slowed down in the aftermath of the shock. Like the long, slow abiding of the Retlaw ruins just behind us.

On Fire for the Rest of My Life

IN 2021, I was westbound in the way that a person can be housebound, or a plant can be rootbound, in the sense of not able to move or grow, or so it felt. It was year two of the COVID-19 pandemic. Travel had slowed to a stop. I was accustomed to taking work trips to central Canada and to the United States a few times each year, and to Europe or Africa every year or two. Recreational travel—holidays abroad, vacations—had never been a large part of my life, but I took for granted that I would always have opportunities to go somewhere. I thought of myself as Pico Iyer's global soul—at home while in motion, belonging not to one place but to a matrix of places that I crossed and recrossed.

This notion of myself as a global soul was a bit of a conceit. With a daughter and job to keep me in Edmonton, I could hardly be a displaced wanderer or a high-flier. But I held on to the idea that I was a person who goes to places that are far away, a person who is not really from here. Then it all changed.

The pandemic made me conscious of my westboundedness, both because I had ground to a halt in Edmonton and because I had become aware that mortality was now more complicated. I did not get acutely sick from the coronavirus, but I was constantly reminded that I could. I was aware of frailty, from the daily death tolls.

Thinking about the physical catastrophes wrought by the virus led me to thoughts of physical decline, specifically mine. I was aware that my own embodied life was moving towards its inevitable conclusion, even as I waited for the pandemic to stop and for real life to begin again. But it kept going on and on, and it seemed as though years of my life would go with it. I began to think I didn't have that much time left, and COVID was using it up.

Each week brought new disappointments, yet the same disappointments kept happening again and again. The government spun its wheels, making the same mistakes over and over: about COVID, about oil, about conspiracy theories, about everything. Comments that I'd put on Facebook in 2020, complaints about the pandemic, kept reappearing a year later, still unfortunately relevant. I had difficulty seeing my present progressing into my future—it was much easier to see myself treading in loops, time going in a circle.

Yet even if I had difficulty imagining my own future, it was all too easy to see (and imagine, when I could not see) the future of the world. It wasn't just the pandemic that brought on mortal thoughts. Since the start of the twenty-first century, the world was, and still is, burning up. My knowledge of climate change was pushing me towards the realization that the world I thought I knew, the world that was always getting better, or at least maintaining its progress, was gone. The world is going to be on fire for the rest of my life. My own unwinding and the unwinding of the world are proceeding together.

In March 2022, the Intergovernmental Panel on Climate Change issued its sixth assessment report. Its conclusions were bleak. There is almost no chance of limiting the human impact on the planet's temperature to a mere increase of 1.5 degrees Celsius, which was the target of the comparatively optimistic mid-2000s. Current trends will raise the average global temperature between 2.5 and 2.7 degrees by the end of the century. Every ecosystem will be affected. Algae will bloom, fresh water will become salinated, and trees will burn. Small island nations like Fiji or the Maldives will be underwater. Other places will become uninhabitable, either because groundwater reservoirs and rivers will dry up, or because it will be too hot for crops to grow, or for people to be outside for more than a few hours. Mount Kilimanjaro will be devoid of ice or snow in less than twenty years. Siberian permafrost is already thawing and collapsing. Once-in-a-century fires and storms will be once-every-couple-of-years within a few decades. The weather systems that controlled the timing of precipitation will dissolve into entropy, exacerbating the impacts of hot soils and dying groundcover in food-growing areas.

Cutting greenhouse gas emissions immediately is the only thing that will help, but that isn't happening, say the authors of the report. Instead, national leaders are drawing up ever more ambitious plans and declarations and commitments, without putting them into action. Or at best, ineffective adaptations are being attempted. These misdirected efforts are exemplified by the state of Florida, where efforts to mitigate climate change have focussed on the construction of more and more elaborate sea walls, all destined to fail in the face of hurricane events and steady sea-level rises.

People my age may live to see some of the report's predicted devastation, but not the worst. Our children will see the worst. Our grandchildren, if we have them, may inherit a chastened world with a population forced to live within its means, but only after a tremendous harrowing. The best-case scenario is a sort of bottleneck or isthmus between now and a healthy, sustainable, low-carbon future; the worst-case scenario is that we burn the whole thing up sometime around 2060.

In Alberta, every year since 1998 has been warmer than the average of all years for the twentieth century. The Climate Atlas of Canada, produced by the Prairie Climate Centre in Winnipeg, has online tools that allow you to define specific scenarios in the short and medium term, to model the local effects of climate change under different conditions. The atlas shows that, under a set of high-carbon assumptions where we don't do anything to reduce emissions, the average number of days over 30 degrees in Edmonton will increase from just under four during the period from 1976 to 2005, to eleven and a half in the short-term future, from 2021 to 2050. Even under an optimistic scenario in which carbon emissions are drastically reduced, the average number of very hot days per year will still increase to ten in the next thirty years.

It could be worse. In Toronto, according to the atlas, the number of days over 30 degrees is set to increase from twelve to somewhere between twenty-eight and forty-seven in 2050 under the high-carbon scenario—the business-as-usual scenario in which greenhouse gases accumulate at current rates. Toronto's average number of "tropical nights"—twenty-four-hour periods when the temperature does not go below 20 degrees Celsius, hampering the human body's ability to cool itself—is set to go from eight per year to twenty-nine per year in the period from 2021 to 2050, and as high as an average of sixty-nine tropical nights per year by 2080. Toronto and other southern Canadian cities will also be more intensely affected than Edmonton by the "urban heat island" phenomenon, in which temperatures in densely populated cities rise higher than surrounding areas with more vegetation coverage. Such cities are also more likely to experience flash floods and high-precipitation storms. And in eastern Canada, the number of days each year that are very favourable for the spread of wildfires is projected to increase by 200 per cent to 300 per cent by the end of the century, as compared to the number of "fire days" in 2010, which will increase the risk of the same kinds of devastating incendiary storms that now mark the west.

I have known all of this in a sort of distant intellectualized way for a long time, like the way that I was aware of the possibility of nuclear war during the 1980s. However, unlike the possible end of the world by nuclear bomb, which was terrifying but remote, the end of the known world by human-caused overheating is sensed, felt, embodied, closer than my own skin, as the temperature creeps up and up through the twenty-first century.

Nuclear apocalypse was a maybe; it was something that could happen, but could also *not* happen. That indeterminacy does not exist for global warming. The changes are already under way—"baked in," as pundits put it, in an unfortunate choice of words. In the freakishly hot July of 2021, the climate catastrophe really hit home, literally, when temperature records were shattered across Alberta.

That explosion of heat also marked the moment when I finally let go of the expectation of spending the rest of my life somewhere else, somewhere more urbane, maybe more sophisticated and more coastal. Such places, I realized, were also likely to be hit by hurricanes and once-in-a-century storms, or submerged by rising oceans. If not destroyed by water and wind, then razed by fire, as lower-latitude destinations spike to unlivable temperatures. Through no conscious decision and with no foresight, I have ended up in one of the few places that may not be ravaged too badly by climate change: northern Alberta.

So here I stay, at least for the foreseeable future. I have been living in Alberta for over twenty years and have finally come round to the recognition that I am not getting out anytime soon. (When I glanced at my handwritten notes on this topic, the word *Edmonton* looked for a moment like *eschaton*, Greek for the end of the world—melodramatic and a bit laughable, but also fitting.)

While I wait for the end of the world, I read a lot about it. At the moment, many people are writing about the emotions associated with the likelihood of climate disaster, the possibility of the end of the world. Among these emotions is solastalgia—a new concept for me. Solastalgia names the feelings of distress and grief caused by living through harmful changes to the environment. Solastalgia is being homesick for a home you're still living in, which can no longer be your home because it's been degraded, and there's more degradation in sight. It seems like the word of the moment for the 2020s, so I was surprised to learn that this neologism was first coined in 2003 by Australian philosopher Glenn Albrecht, who applied it to drought and open-pit mining in New South Wales.

A 2019 survey of the academic literature on solastalgia found, perhaps predictably, that the term has become more and more common as the years go by. The number of scholarly papers published in 2018 alone about solastalgia was nearly a fifth of all such papers ever published. The research on solastalgia covers an extraordinary range of events, from the acute, sharp-shock crises of war and natural disasters to the slow-moving catastrophes of deforestation and landscape destruction. Solastalgia-themed art projects seem to be everywhere in the early 2020s, from a display of book art in Minneapolis to a tour by Australian pop singer Missy Higgins to a plethora of blogs, online exhibits, and artistic manifestos centred on grief, loss, and sorrow.

Britt Wray's *Generation Dread: Finding Purpose in an Age of Climate Crisis* explores these emotions as experienced by individuals, from enhanced death awareness to existential anxiety to hopelessness. As I read it, I started to remember a concept from my grad-school days in sociology, that of terror management, which refers to the idea that humans are constantly preoccupied with warding off the awareness that we are all going to die. Terror management theory has been around since the 1970s, but I was not at all surprised to encounter it in Wray's book, in the chapter where she discusses climate grief.

My academic, intellectual response to the book—*This sounds like terror management theory; wasn't that originally Becker 1973?*—felt somehow inappropriate. Why was a conceptual genealogy of the term the first thing that came to mind? Was I not *feeling* enough? Was this citational response a way of distancing myself from what was denoted, the overwhelming and irreducible grief? Am I substituting reading about solastalgia for actually experiencing it?

This sense of being almost too far removed from the climate crisis was intensified by reading Lisa Wells's *Believers: Making a Life at the End of the World* and Joanna Pocock's *Surrender: The Call of the American West*. Both are first-person accounts of encounters with people, mainly environmental activists of different stripes, who are gripped by a sense of loss. They're the ones out there in the mud and the rainstorms, transplanting the camas lilies in northwest Oregon, remediating the earth sterilized by wildfires in Southern California, practising ancestral skills for harvesting bison. Pocock meets an urban "rewilder" in Portland, Oregon, who speaks of the importance of "keeping the grief flowing" rather than becoming numb or distracted. By that standard, their grief is active and energized, and mine is not. Is that what I am, numb or distracted?

Not quite. I seem to be at a moment prior to the onslaught of grief, perhaps prior to the full realization that grief, howling or crying or collapsing, might be a proportionate response to what is happening.

I've encountered this moment-before-the-moment feeling before, notably when I revisited one of my first experiences with end-of-the-world literature, Joan Didion's *Slouching Towards Bethlehem*.

Apocalyptic in tone as well as in substance, Didion's famous collection of essays reflects the disintegration and incoherence she saw around her in late-1960s California, from acid-trippers to extreme libertarians to an upwardly mobile spouse-killer.

At a remove of more than forty years, these preoccupations seem almost quaint. *Is that all you've got for the centre not holding and the awakening of dark forces and so on? A bunch of people acting weird in Southern California?* But something of Didion's careful distancing from the disjointedness around her feels familiar, something that could be irony or a preternaturally calm version of shock, but not apathy or torpor. She didn't put the pieces together to lay out a coherent theory of why things were coming apart. She just noted that it was happening. In the poem by W.B. Yeats from which her collection takes its title, the "rough beast" that slouches towards Bethlehem is not born yet; it's a presence that is not entirely present yet. At the time Didion wrote her essays, she may not have been able to articulate the centrifugal forces pulling at her world, sending the pieces flying everywhere. And neither can I.

Rossdale Flats and the Bomb Shelter

MY ATTACHMENT TO THE WEST has grown over the last two decades, like a seed I didn't plant that took root anyway. That attachment is both sharpened and deepened by consciousness of my own mortality and the disastrous heating of the planet. Because of both mortalities, the number of places that I will come to know is finite. I had better learn to love, or like, or at least appreciate these places that I'm in, because they are what's been given to me to hold on to in my final few decades. If I don't learn to inhabit the west, I don't have an alternative.

But not all places in the west are equally compelling. At this point in my life, I'm drawn to places that are not what they once were. More precisely, I'm attracted by the ruins, where things are fading away or are disappearing entirely, leaving only remnants and outlines. Most of the place-knowledge that I've acquired in the last few years is about these ruins in the west, both the ones that are obvious and inescapable and the ones that are hidden in plain sight—or not-so-plain sight, off the paved road and down a few trails.

< *Bomb shelter, built in 1953, just west of downtown Edmonton, Alberta.*
(*Photo by the author.*)

Not everything that happened a long time ago is a ruin today. The past is not always dead, as Barack Obama observed in 2008, quoting William Faulkner who might have been quoting someone else, and sometimes it's not even past. Sometimes what happened long ago is history, but not ruin—in other words, sometimes the past is so durable that we can't ever say it's over. For the distinction between history and ruin, I think of two places in Edmonton, about five kilometres from each other: the Rossdale flats and the bomb shelter.

The site that's known today as the Rossdale power plant, right at the river's edge, was once a burying ground. The remains of at least thirty men, women, and children, who died when Edmonton was a trading fort in the mid-nineteenth century, were found when portions of the power plant lands were excavated in the early twenty-first century.

However, the use of this land as a final resting ground for human bodies is only one link in a chain of continuous usage that stretches back for millennia, and forward for—who knows how long? Archaeologists have found evidence that people were using this site for at least eight thousand years, maybe longer. They fished, hunted beaver, camped, and traded. According to some accounts, the area around the bends in the North Saskatchewan River that is now Edmonton was a pêhonân (Cree for "a place of waiting for other people")—although some say the pêhonân designation doesn't fit Edmonton's location and its application to the site is an anachronism.

In 1802, white traders built a fort in the flats, which was used until 1830 when trading activities were moved to a bluff overlooking the river. It was a trading fort until 1891, and then appears to have gradually fallen into disrepair until 1915, when it was dismantled. In 1902, the first electricity-generating station was built on the original fort site, hard by the river, and in 1930, the present building went up. The Rossdale power plant was expanded six times over the next three decades, each expansion marked by a new cornerstone as it spread out gradually across the flats. The power plant started reducing its output in the 1990s and was decommissioned in 2011. Somewhere along the way, the whole area came to be called Rossdale, after white settler Donald Ross, who arrived from Scotland in 1872. In one of those historical ironies that seems too perfect to be true, Ross gained renown by running Edmonton's first hotel, consisting of a couple of rooms on the second floor of his house that he rented out to the transient: the impermanent white settlers.

In the full sweep of human time in the flats, the power plant and Donald Ross's hotel and even the burial grounds represent only a brief burst of activity, the moments of arrival and vanishing close at hand. But Rossdale, the river flats, with its unused power plant and its graves, is not a ruin. It's been occupied and used for centuries, and there's every reason to believe that Rossdale as a place of human action will go on and on. The use that humans make of the location may change, but the site itself will probably always be peopled.

Then there's the bomb shelter. Actually, there are several bomb shelters in Edmonton: a few that are known to the public and more that are private, in the back yards of homes built during the Cold War. Edmonton is a relatively small city and not near any crucial port, but at the start of the Cold War it was also the opening point of the land route to Alaska, which meant, with a bit of imagination, the beginning of the crossover to Russian territory. As the Cold War wore on and oil became more and more important, Edmonton acquired some strategic significance because of its refineries, storage tanks, and pipeline terminals. This led to the construction of a big civil defence shelter in the Mackenzie Ravine, just west of downtown.

This shelter, or bunker, was meant to serve as a command post for city officials if Edmonton were hit by a Soviet-launched nuclear bomb. In 1953, the year the bunker was built, this was not an entirely far-fetched worry. The bunker could house up to thirty-six people for fourteen days—long enough, as the thinking of the time went, to avoid the worst effects of radioactive fallout. It was equipped with sleeping, bathing, cooking, and broadcasting facilities.

The full history of this bunker is unknown. At some point—no one seems to know when—city staff stopped maintaining it. It became a hangout for local kids who were liberal with their graffiti until, at some other point—again, no one seems to know—the bunker was sealed and locked. City documents from the 2010s refer to a plan to unseal the structure in order to renovate or restore it, but so far, nothing seems to have happened.

In 2010, local photographer and civil defence enthusiast Fred Armbruster got permission from the city to unlock the doors and look around. His photographs reveal what you might expect of a Cold War haunted house: mildew and rust stains on the walls, square rooms bathed in orange light with 1950s-era tables and desks built into the walls, and oddly homey-looking toilets and sinks. The geometric pattern on the old linoleum is still faintly visible. For me, a child of the 1970s and 1980s, seeing these photos was like seeing the interiors of my postwar elementary schools, with just a hint of mission-command aesthetic. Everything that could be pulled out had been removed— furniture, fixtures, wires. After Armbruster's visit and a brief bit of publicity in the local paper and TV news, the bunker was resealed and remains today a concrete cube protruding from the side of a valley in what was an inner-ring suburb in the 1950s.

The bunker is ruined. It once had a utility, a connection to bigger projects of economics and politics, and then that connection was severed. It is a remainder of what it once was. The mortmain, the dead hand of the past, holds the place. In the bunker, history takes the shape of entropy. In the Rossdale flats, by contrast, history takes the shape of constant transformation, which is neither constant improvement nor constant degradation, but is something close to life.

The West
and Its Ruins

IN *A FIELD GUIDE TO GETTING LOST*, Rebecca Solnit says that ruins are in the same relation to inhabited places as the unconscious is to the conscious mind: "Ruins become the unconscious of a city, its memory, unknown, darkness, lost lands, and in this truly bring it to life." What she says of the city is also true of the economic apparatus of the west, which for over a hundred years has been growing and entangling, sprouting pseudopods of towns or farms or mines or bridges and then casting them off when the next opportunity for extraction arises.

Anthropologist Anna Lowenhaupt Tsing gets a bit more specific, identifying what she calls "capitalist ruins": places and landscapes that were once functional for the accumulation of capital, but are no longer usable, or at least not usable in the ways their builders had imagined. You could also think of capitalist ruins as places that are beyond the threshold of commodification, from which no financial value can be extracted any longer.

Both Solnit and Tsing agree that ruins are not dead space. They point to an absence, not a void. They are what is left behind, but they still have some kind of life. At the very least, they live in the imaginations of the wanderers who come across them.

Part of the settler mythology of the West, capital W, is that there are not supposed to be ruins here. The settler west is new, it's the future, it's where tomorrow begins. The late nineteenth- and early twentieth-century posters encouraging transatlantic immigration to the North-West Territories, and later to Alberta and Saskatchewan, made use of the iconography of the sunrise, the springtime, the new day's opportunity to slough off the old economic constraints of Europe and build a future. Of the Canadian territories, Alberta in particular was billed as the Last Best West. As a result, most non-Indigenous people here have shallow roots—three generations in the west is enough to qualify settler families as having been here "forever," especially in some rural communities.

The mystique of the frontier for white people holds that the settlers are always just arriving: the homesteads are rising up from the prairie, the roads are unfurling, and the boomtowns are booming. It came as something of a surprise, therefore, once I really started to look at the place, to realize how much abandonment had already happened. The remains of many futures are scattered across the plains and the forests, the badlands and the foothills.

In the dominant political story of Alberta, as told by settlers, the province is figured as the future, the place where tomorrow begins, fuelled (literally) by endless expansion of coal and oil and gas exploitation; the place where the cities get torn down and rebuilt with every carbon-based economic boom.

For most of the inhabited history of the west, the people who lived here built things that returned to the earth. The university where I work, the University of Alberta, is home to the Institute of Prairie and Indigenous Archaeology, which teaches twenty-first century westerners about the ones who went before them. The discipline of archaeology, especially Indigenous archaeology, is no longer about pulling things out of the ground or digging up the evidence of people who were once here, or who have been here continuously for thousands of years.

If I were trained as an archaeologist today, I would know how to use non-invasive techniques to read the world around me as a text of human history, to see the chimney that's buried under a few metres of earth or the forest garden tended for generations, hidden in plain sight in a stand of native perennial plants (*Archaeologies of the Heart*, co-edited by Dr. Kisha Supernant of the IPIA, opened this world to me). As a non-archaeologist, however, the traces of the past are limited to the things that I can see with my un-trained, not-Indigenous eyes: buildings, roads, railway tracks, abandoned creations of concrete and metal and wood. This particular built history of Alberta that has survived until now is pretty scanty, which means that finding the things that have been abandoned in the west takes more work than it would farther east.

The cycles of building and abandonment have also been uneven across the west. If you're starting in the middle of Alberta or Saskatchewan or British Columbia, the farther south you go towards the American border, the more ghost towns and random outposts you'll find, most having risen and fallen as demand for coal rose and fell. By the time oil took over as the main resource being pulled from the ground, extractive technologies had changed, and little towns no longer needed to be built every few miles to house the drillers and miners, or to service the railroads that carried the coal.

Farther north, around Westlock and Cold Lake and Slave Lake and Barrhead, there are fewer ghost towns but more abandoned buildings, mainly former farmhouses that fell into disuse as farms consolidated and smallholdings were swallowed up by bigger players. On many stretches of road, such as Highway 63 from Newbrook to Fort Saskatchewan, the number of abandoned dwellings rivals the number of houses that are still inhabited.

My interest in these ruins is Romantic, capital R, in part. I know this as Romance because I feel the sentimental strings plucked by the aesthetics of decay. I think of the images that Google pulls up for the term "modern ruins"—the old farmhouse in the field of grass, the crumbling gas station with one light on, and, if I go back a few centuries, the falling-down castle at the edge of the cliff, at midnight, overlooking a raging sea. My imagination is caught by the presence of the absence of the powers that built these things and then moved on. Gas stations and farmhouses are not exactly Shelley's statue of Ozymandias, but also not completely different. What do we no longer see? What forces, human or otherwise, made their mark and disappeared, leaving behind testimony to the evanescent nature of, well, everything?

My interest in the ruins is also partly forensic. Something was here and now it's not. People were doing something in this place and then they stopped. The span of time separating them from me can never be known for sure, but the fact of that separation is compelling. *What happened here? Is this a crime scene? Who did it?* I'm fascinated by these places for the same reasons that I'm fascinated by mummies and skeletons, the remains of bodies where life used to be.

Each year, the United Nations climate change conferences highlight the potential for ruin on a much larger scale. Even if the member nations won't make the changes that must be made to slow down the heating and the eventual disinhabitation of the planet, I can tell which way the wind is blowing, and it is not in the direction of the industries that Albertan governments have staked their fortunes on for most of the last hundred years. This is a fitting time to look for the ruins of the west, as the entire province turns into the aftermath of extraction, a giant former boomtown, the proliferating ruins of a carbon-based economy.

Ruins, almost by definition, don't have many people in them. This does not mean that the ruins I visit are unpeopled. Within these ruins, I encounter traces of people who had once been there, or of people who occupy adjacent real estate in my imagination—including many writers, some who are still alive and writing today, and others who are long gone. I can't enter into dialogue with these people, but I can hear their voices in my west.

The ruins of human habitation are interleaved with the more-than-human world. Being westbound also means being in the same place as enormous flocks of birds, glacial rapids, golden tamarack, hoodoos. They are reclaiming some of the ruins, they are bordering others. They will inhabit the ruins that are still to come.

GRIZZLY TRAIL
PROMOTIONAL ASSOCIATION

CENTRE OF ALBERTA
L.S. 14-33-63-7-W5

HONORARY CHAIRMAN
KEN KOWALSKI M.L.A.

SURVEYED BY
ROY CHIMIUK

JULY 1989

Swan Hills

TO GET TO SWAN HILLS FROM EDMONTON, take the old Klondike Trail, now Highway 33. The trail was surveyed in 1897 by Thomas Chalmers, a surveyor working for the North-West Territorial government, and built the following year. Chalmers was tasked with finding the shortest and fastest overland route to the Yukon gold fields, one that would enable prospectors to bypass Alaska and stay on Canadian soil. The Chalmers route looked simple on the map, but was neither short nor fast in reality. Chalmers hadn't reckoned on the muskeg bogs or the elevation changes as the trail climbed up and down the Swan Hills. He also had not sought permission or advice from the Cree who passed through the area regularly as they travelled for hunting, which might have saved the road-clearing party some of the backbreaking work of cutting a trail.

The white prospectors who followed Chalmers expected to reach the gold within a few weeks, but found nowhere to rest on the trail, nowhere to stop and feed their horses. Historian Pierre Berton estimated that only a fifth of the eight hundred gold migrants who set out on the trail made it to the Klondike, and that two thousand horses belonging to their parties died as they travelled. The old trail was abandoned within five years of its construction. I am told by friends who do a lot of backcountry hiking that the ruts where wagon wheels

< *Cairn marking the centre of the province, near Swan Hills, Alberta.*

(*Photo by awmcphee, courtesy of Wikimedia Commons, licensed under* CC BY-SA 4.0.

https://en.wikipedia.org/wiki/Swan_Hills#/media/File:Centre_of_Alberta_cairn.jpg)

got stuck in the mud are still visible in some parts of the pine forest that covers the hills.

My partner and I travelled Highway 33 in 2017, on a road trip to see what we could see northwest of Edmonton. The land began to undulate about a hundred kilometres from the city. We were slowed by trucks carrying oilfield equipment as they lumbered up and down the inclines, and we had to dodge out of the radius of loaded logging trucks as they turned slowly on the curves. The hill country rolled on and on, thick with pine and poplar, dotted with small oil wells about the height of a person. The surroundings were beautiful, but lacked the glamour and iconic vistas of the Rockies to the south or the vastness of the subarctic regions to the north.

At the midpoint of what used to be the trail is now a settlement. Swan Hills, the town, is the geographic middle of Alberta. There's a cairn marking the dead centre of the province, at 54 degrees north and 115 degrees west, about a ten-minute drive south of the township. We were surprised to learn that the town is not as old as the trail—it's only a bit younger than I am, brought into existence by a joint venture between the Alberta government and the oil companies, when petroleum deposits were discovered around Lesser Slave Lake. The community's website celebrates Swan Hills' hopes for prosperity through oil, proclaiming that "there's nothing like an oil boom to help build a town!" Swan Hills, according to these anonymous civic boosters, is archetypal Alberta: a "town full of the opportunity that has always characterized the west."

But Swan Hills today is on its way to ghost town status, drained of jobs and commerce by downturns in the oil and gas industry. The central retail strip has far more parking spaces than are warranted by the three or four shops still hanging on. According to census data, the population declined by 11 per cent between 2006 and 2011, and by another 11 per cent between 2011 and 2016. It was home to about 1,300 people when we visited. Only 10 per cent of the population has an undergraduate degree. Four of the seventy-nine businesses registered in the town closed in 2019. The biggest employer in Swan Hills is not an oil and gas company; it's a disposal facility that receives hazardous chemical waste from other communities across Canada. The plant burns and dissolves the PCB-laden materials and buries them in the ground at a specially constructed landfill.

The Swan Hills Waste Treatment Centre opened in 1987. Nine years later an incinerator malfunctioned, sending polychlorinated biphenyls and other contaminants into the air. The provincial government issued health advisories warning against eating game meat or fish caught within a thirty-kilometre radius of the plant. For the Sucker Creek, Driftpile, and Swan River First Nations north of the facility, these warnings, combined with Elders' observations that wild plants looked different after the chemical leak, led to the disruption of "country food" practices centred on the land. Some families shied away from returning to their traditional camping and hunting places.

By 2012, the concentrations of pollutants in the bodies of deer and trout had declined, but were still so high that the health advisory was revised to a fifteen-kilometre radius, rather than being dropped completely. The waste treatment centre is set to be closed completely by 2025.

In the interim, Swan Hills doesn't seem to be thriving. When my partner and I stopped there to pick up coffee on our 2017 road trip, it was almost impossible for me not to imagine abandonment. Coming off the highway, we found a lopsided pentagon in what was likely intended to be the central plaza of the town. The middle of the pentagon was an empty parking lot, surrounded by the two-storey, brown-and-white commercial buildings typical of many other northern towns. Most of the stores were vacant or boarded up; of those that were still going concerns, only the liquor store attached to a disused motel and a small grocery were open. We bought our coffee from a machine in the grocery. The only activity in the store was in a back corner holding a bin of used DVDs, apparently castoffs from the movie rental places that were closing all over the country as internet streaming services started to take over. A couple of teenagers poked through the bin looking for horror movies and came up triumphantly with *Sorority Girl Massacre*. The sun was setting, turning the dirty snow blue.

Westbound
All Along

THE WEST IS NEW TERRITORY FOR ME, as a person who is a descendant of ancestors as well as an individual with my own life story. I don't come from western people. My ancestors on both parents' sides, as far as I can trace, are slightly different shades of pale white settlers, both branches securely attached to the eastern half of North America.

My father's distant ancestors arrived in Massachusetts in 1637. For European settlers in those days, the western frontier meant what is now upstate New York. My many-times-great-grandfathers took part in a military operation against the original inhabitants of that part of the world—commonly known as King Philip's War, also known as the first instance of "ethnic cleansing" in colonial America. After the American Revolution, they settled into farming in New Hampshire and Massachusetts and fishing off the coast of Maine.

My mother's ancestors came to Canada more recently, in the nineteenth century, and from a more northerly part of the British Isles than my father's people. They never strayed west of the Huron County region around Hamilton and London, the part of southwestern Ontario associated with the fiction of Alice Munro. They were teachers, mostly; a few were members of the clergy or small business owners. They emphasized responsibility, thrift, common sense, and doing good for others, in a low-key Methodist way. Despite a general tendency towards modesty and keeping oneself to oneself, these settler families did produce a generation of missionaries in the early twentieth century. Among them were my maternal grandparents, who travelled west across Canada, the farthest west anyone in their families had ever been, to embark on a steamship journey from Vancouver to Shanghai in the 1930s.

Except for the missionaries, as far as I know, neither side of the family partook in any romantic notion of a frontier, nor did they feel the need to go west. They were rooted in southern Ontario and New England, where the very place names echoed the wellspring of Anglo-Saxon Protestant culture across the Atlantic.

My immediate family, however, did go west after a fashion. Before we settled in Toronto, my father's employer moved its middle-management staff every couple of years. My early childhood memories involve a succession of places we were either moving into or out of.

The last place before Toronto was Texas, where we lived for three years in what was then a smallish town and is now part of the greater Houston sprawl. I remember tract-house bungalows on curving streets, each with one or two low-slung American-made boatlike cars, and humidity that melted stunned transplants from the north, botanical and animal, into torpid immobility. I recall drooping mulberry trees, and a pervasive gender conformity that expressed itself, in my eyes, in frilly Holly Hobbie sundresses and baton-twirling lessons for girls. It was southern and suburban and seventies, a place where the questing and idealistic years of the 1960s might never have happened.

Overlaying these enervating memories of daily life, however, is the family vacation we took one winter to the Big Bend region of west Texas. I remember stopping at the viaduct bridge over the Pecos River and experiencing my first encounter with immensity when I peered through the gaps in the rusty guardrail at the river, impossibly far below. (At 323 feet above the water, the original Pecos bridge was the third highest in the world when it was built in 1892.)

We stopped there because my parents wanted to see all that space, the heights and the depths of it. I sensed that they wanted their three children to remain safely in the car, but also wanted us to see it too. While my mother was occupied with my two younger brothers, I ducked around her, drawn like a magnet to the abyss beyond the safety fence.

It was vast in all directions—above me, below me, the flat desert stretching out before me and behind me. A decade later, when I read the English Romantic poets as an undergraduate and learned about the notion of the sublime, my first association was to the Pecos viaduct.

When we reached our destination at Big Bend National Park, I saw reddish boulders the size of houses, which seemed to have pushed their way out of the earth. I saw the remains of a volcano. I saw tumbleweed moving as though under its own power across dry fields spotted with sage. I saw the ruins of a cabin with walls a foot thick to keep out the worst of the summer heat. Those walls stood only about as high as my nine-year-old head, which didn't seem to fit any adult I had ever seen. The roof and the beams of the house were long gone. I wondered for the first time what it would be like to abandon a life, to pick up what you could carry and walk away from a house you had built. I wondered what it would be like to live with next to no water, if the river ran dry and the old well returned your bucket empty.

That same day, or perhaps another day, we visited the big river itself, the Rio Grande. We climbed down through passes in the ochre canyon walls to reach water that was flat and still, biscuit-coloured and shallow. I looked across it to Mexico, thinking, *That is another country*, trying out the idea of foreignness and strangeness, moving the words around in my mind. The US-Mexico border, in the form of the Rio Grande, was the first time I had seen the delineation between where I belonged and where I might not belong. I tried to reconcile the foreignness of the other side with the knowledge it was also so close that I could toss a stick into the river and the current would carry it there.

In the early 1970s, the border was not the militarized danger zone that it became in later decades, and perhaps I could have even waded into the muddy waters and swum to Mexico, utilizing the hours of swimming lessons I'd undergone back in Houston. As a middle-class white Anglo child growing up in Texas, I had acquired an exoticized image of Mexico as a place where everyone wore embroidered white blouses, and the ancient pyramids of the Aztecs sprouted from arid plains. It was hard for me to grasp that I was looking at that very place, right across the river from where I stood.

Strangeness and extremity, places without people, or places with no people anymore, straight lines off to the horizon of water and earth and vegetation—thinking of these childhood memories, perhaps I have been westbound since early in my life.

Campus
Saint-Jean

ON THE SECOND-LAST DAY OF JUNE 2021, I'm sitting behind the main red-brick building of Campus Saint-Jean, the French language offshoot of the University of Alberta. Edmonton is in the grip of a heat wave. There's a little bit of shade under an oak tree (a rarity in a city whose canopy is mainly elms and poplars). The coolest spot here is probably the Lourdes grotto attached to the building—an oval of concrete roughly the height of a person, with a statue of Mary and a plaque about the devotion of one particular long-deceased Oblate friar. Formerly known as the university's Faculté Saint-Jean, this campus has been here for just over a hundred years. It began as the juniorate of the Oblate order of missionary priests, where young white franco-phone men trained for the priesthood.

The Oblates are in the news this summer and not for a good reason. They ran forty-eight of the country's 139 Indian residential schools, in which abuse and neglect of the Indigenous children in their care was rife. For weeks I've been reading about the grounds of these old, now-shuttered schools: the invisible hollows under the sod that indicate unmarked graves, the indentations in the land that show where the children were put, the harm that was done for many more years than I've been alive.

< *Statue of Frère Anthony Kowalczyk, by sculptor Danek Mozdzenski, at Campus Saint-Jean, University of Alberta, Edmonton.* (Photo by the author.)

43

I've been in 40-degree-plus heat in Zimbabwe and South Sudan and Uganda, but I've never been this hot this far north in Canada. Neither has anyone else. It's much drier in northern Alberta than it was in central Africa, so the occasional hint of a breeze makes a great difference, unlike the relentless wet stillness of African hot-season air. This is not the Alberta that I've known before now. The mismatch between what I see, the soft green community garden and the grounds of Campus Saint-Jean, and what I feel, the invisible fog of the heat, is jarring. These experiences—Alberta summers and blasting heat—have never overlapped for me before.

I have been reading recently about the heat dome effect, and how it's currently crushing parts of British Columbia. It's happening because the western part of the Pacific is heating faster than the eastern part. Trade winds push the hot air east, and extreme oscillations in the high altitude of the jet stream cause portions of the stream to get stuck over large chunks of the continent, forming a lid that presses the warm air beneath it down. The compression exacerbates the heat and voilà, the sky becomes a convection oven.

I know that human activity did this. This is what a climate catastrophe looks like in its slow-moving form, much slower than wildfires or a storm surge. I know this is going to keep happening, as are global health crises, of which COVID-19 is the most recent but not the last. I have to get used to pandemics of novel pathogens and I have to get used to the overwhelming heat. As I sit here in the shade, I hear emergency vehicle sirens from Whyte Avenue several blocks to the south, so much more frequent these days because of the pandemic as well as the number of people felled by heat stroke. The wailing rise and fall reinforces my sense that this emergency, this multi-layered catastrophe, is going to go on for a long time.

This is the truth I'm headed into. The period of my own life marked by decline is happening on a planet tilting rapidly into destruction. People of my cohort—born in the 1960s and 1970s, North Americans, white and middle-class—may have lived through the last good times on our planet, the last summers that didn't kill, the last years when the forests didn't burn in May. It's the height of pathetic fallacy to liken individual aging to climate change, but today it feels like the planet and I are falling out of order together.

| What I didn't know on June 29, 2021, is that the next day would be the second hottest ever recorded in Edmonton. That day came in the midst of the longest stretch of days exceeding 30 degrees in Edmonton's recorded history. Six months later, on December 27, 2021, the weather station at the Edmonton International Airport hit minus 42 degrees, the lowest temperature ever recorded there. Record after record, extreme after extreme.

I'm reading Elisa Gabbert's essay "Magnificent Desolation," about the thrills people get from disaster, and thinking that she's right. Record after record, extreme after extreme—there is a sort of awful excitement to be heard in news reports and online chatter. *How hot is it going to be? How bad will it get?* Maybe we're primed for this episode of climate disaster because we're in the middle of another once-in-a-lifetime catastrophe, the global coronavirus pandemic. But why is it horribly thrilling? Why is this hopped-up excitement a response to disaster? What is it about all-time records—the hottest, the wettest, the worst—that there's gratification in breaking them, whatever they are? Why is it exhilarating to know that we're heading into uncharted territory?

Maybe it's not so much excitement as it is a weird sort of relief, to be arriving for real in the prophesied dystopian future, to be able to say to ourselves, *This is what it's going to be like; this is what it feels like to be living in the new territory of climate catastrophe.* We have arrived, we are here, wherever "here" will turn out to be.

The End of the World and the Ends of the Earth

WHAT HAPPENS AT THE END OF THE EARTH? I'm looking at two books that ask that question, both collections of essays by heavy-hitter middlebrow American commentators: Jonathan Franzen's 2018 volume *The End of the End of the Earth* and Robert Kaplan's book from twenty years earlier, 1997's *The Ends of the Earth: From Togo to Turkmenistan, from Iran to Cambodia, a Journey to the Frontiers of Anarchy*. And what a difference two decades make.

For Kaplan, the ends of the earth are exotic geographies. His "frontiers of anarchy" are near enough to serve as alarming possibilities but far enough that the American reader in 1997 could think, *Well, it's not happening to me, it's not happening here, if the end is coming, it's not coming tomorrow*. He located the ends of the earth in places experiencing war and devastation, far from western Europe and North America—from Togo to Turkmenistan, as the subtitle says. (Kaplan did write *An Empire Wilderness: Travels into America's Future* two years later, in which he chronicled environmental destruction and political apathy throughout the United States, so I can't say he's entirely wrapped up in the exotic other.)

Franzen, by contrast, locates the end of the earth not *out there*, but everywhere. He goes birding in Antarctica and off the coast of California;

he and his girlfriend take a safari trip to east Africa. But for him, the ends of the earth are not places. The real ends of the earth, he says, are the things that are ending—the demise of bird species all over the world, for example, or the demise of American political optimism (a demise that began with 9/11 and blasted into orbit with the election of Trump in 2016). Franzen's book was published before the January 6, 2021, mob attack on the US Capitol, but that would certainly fit into this trajectory of crescendoing crises.

His real subject, however, is the destruction of the physical environment. This will harm the birds he loves so much and bring other forms of life to an end as well. Franzen is not convinced that climate change is the biggest threat—he holds that the eradication of biodiversity and habitats is much worse—but the end of the earth is much more immediate for him than for Kaplan. Kaplan offers object lessons, tinged with no small amount of ethnocentricity, in how not to govern large countries; Franzen urges us to try to save the small things we love, because attempting to save anything bigger than our personal passions is futile. We are already on the road to too many degrees of warming, the bird of hope has flown away, the horse is out of the barn, and the train is accelerating down the wrong track to the edge of the cliff. Nobody's going to throw the switch that diverts the trolley.

The end of the earth is a prediction and a metaphor. I speculate that the phrase originated with early European cartography, before globes came into use to represent the round ball of the planet. Maps rendered the known world as a flat, two-dimensional rectangle; every direction came to an end defined by the edges of the medium on which the map was drawn. This brings to mind "the round earth's imagined corners" in Donne's *Holy Sonnets*. In one particular sonnet, Donne pictures something close to what we might call the end of the world—the moment when God's creation comes to fruition, when all is reconciled and resolved in the resurrection of the dead and the fulfillment of prophecy. At that apocalyptic time, which exists outside of ordinary time, Donne sees angels on the edges of the earth, blowing their trumpets as they move towards the centre, with "numberless infinities" of souls liberated from death preceding them. For Donne the holy man, the reformed dissolute, this was the end of the world.

The ends of the earth, in colloquial secular use today, refers to somewhere that is far away, not here, a measure of travel extended almost to an infinite horizon. Someone who would go to the ends of the earth is a very, very dedicated person. The phrase has a bit of a fairy-tale ring, of half-remembered stories about princesses and heroes. As someone forever beguiled by the possibilities of somewhere-else-not-here, the idea of going to the ends of the earth for any reason has an intuitive appeal for me.

In Edmonton, there's an overlook above a ravine where teenagers used to congregate away from adult eyes, to smoke and drink and drop small appliances over the edge to the banks of the river far below. For years it was known informally as the End of the World, allegedly because it was so hard for parents and other responsible adults to find; also because one wrong step would send you fifteen metres down to the riverbank. The name eventually became so well known that even people like me, who were never teenagers in Edmonton, knew about it. It even found its way onto Google Maps.

In 2018, the city parks department came in and cleaned it up, posting signs advising of an 11:00 p.m. curfew. The site was given the less evocative but more historically correct name of Keillor Point, after Fredrick Keillor, a white settler physician who came to Edmonton after the First World War and bought up the fertile land along the former road leading to the river valley. The End of the World is now a prime location for dog walkers and selfie-takers, especially when the sun is setting.

"The end of the world" is rarely stated explicitly in the news, but it's an unspoken possibility, an idea that lurks behind so much of what gets reported. Fires, floods, mudslides, killing heat, worst-ever blizzards— is it even possible that this is *not* the end of the world? If I speculate in this direction, I'm entering the realm of hyperbole, because the world— the planet—will not come to an end. Even if *Homo sapiens* wipes itself out, we can't completely sterilize the soil and the water, and something or someone will survive.

Whatever is coming won't be worse than the most recent mass extinction event, sixty-six million years ago. The Cretaceous–Tertiary event, in which the aftermath of an asteroid crashing into Earth acidified the oceans and stopped photosynthesis by blotting out the sun, resulted in the death of somewhere north of half of all living creatures, including the dinosaurs. Some geologists claim that the asteroid landed on a bed of gypsum, and the impact sent clouds of sulphur into the sky, which led to a torrent of acid rain all over the planet. A geological marker of the event, known as the K–T boundary, is visible as a thin line of rock in the badlands and deserts of central and southern Alberta.

We think there was no intelligent life—at least not as we know it—before the Cretaceous–Tertiary event. I always assumed that dinosaurs, being reptiles with small skulls relative to body size, must have been dumb. I never entertained the possibility of dinosaur language, or dinosaur culture, or dinosaur thought. The devastation caused by the asteroid strike was so great that it would have wiped out any built structures or artifacts. But might those things have been possible? Could dinosaurs have been aware that their world was ending, conscious of the skies with no sun, or of the deluge of acid rain? Did those dinosaurs who lived far from the ancient coasts know about the giant tsunamis? Is it arrogant to assume that these reptiles must have died ignorant of their condition?

These vast spans of time remind me of the final chapters of H.G. Wells's *The Time Machine*, in which the unnamed time traveller arrives millions of years in the future, when humans are gone. Earth's sun is huge and red and possibly dying. Mercury looms in the night sky because the planets have shifted in their orbits. But even there, on a rocky beach, the time traveller is surrounded by enormous crabs, alive and moving but insentient, waving their antennae at him in reflex.

Even though the world won't soon end in a planetary sense, I fear that it is likely to end in a human sense. My world—my experiences and the ideas that I have about them, the real or imagined communities that I share them with, the currents of change and transformation that I live through—will certainly end, probably in about thirty years. But overlaid on the knowledge of my own eventual demise is the knowledge that the world might come to an end for everybody, either around the time of my own expiry or shortly thereafter. I might belong to one of the last generations. (I am unlikely to ever know if this is true, because even the most devastating climate change prophecies still put the end of civilization several decades out, long after I will have departed.)

This does not mean that the present, as we stare down the barrel of the end of the world, is the worst time to be alive. According to the internet, the honour of the Worst Year Ever goes to 536 CE, in which one or possibly two volcanoes erupted, wiping out harvests from China to Europe to Peru. Temperatures plunged around the world and did not recover for a century. The bubonic plague broke out and killed a third of the population of the Byzantine Empire. Wars and chaos followed. The change in the sun, obscured by volcanic ash, was seen as a portent of doom, the displeasure of the gods. For the people alive then, the world may very well have been ending.

When I teach undergraduate sociology, I talk about social and cultural generations, and how history differentiates one from another. One truism from this scholarship in North America is the idea that the post–Baby Boom age cohort—Generation X—was the first generation in centuries who could expect to have less money and a lower standard of living than their parents. This has not been true for me personally, thanks to a tenure-protected faculty job as a professor. But even if mine is the first downwardly mobile generation relative to our parents and grandparents, our own descendants will have it even worse. They may be the first generation to grow up in a world that is getting worse and worse by every indicator, not just the personal-finance ones.

In my lifetime, demographic indicators such as life expectancy and child mortality have been heading in the right directions in many places—proof that some projects of world-betterment bore fruit, at least for a time. But now I see them flipping around and going backwards, one by one, place by place. Take, for example, the downward trend in life expectancies for men in the former Soviet Union, brought on by too much vodka and heroin after the switch from centralized socialism to kleptocratic capitalism rendered them superfluous; the spread of HIV and AIDS in southern Africa and Asia, driven by economic inequality and the low value of black and brown lives to the most powerful interests in the postcolonial world; and the much-ballyhooed decline in life expectancy among white American men (who not so long ago were the masters of the universe), driven by drug use and chronic illnesses, so-called deaths of despair. As the mortality bills from COVID began to come due, life expectancy for all Americans, not just the white men, has slid by nearly three years between 2019 and 2021.

No wonder dystopian fiction is the literary genre of the moment. And no wonder I sometimes crave it, and other times I can barely stand to read it because it brings on a sense of dread mixed with shame, eclipsing the magnificence of the desolation. The dread is because the scenarios in this genre could all happen—no water, no food, mass deaths—and the shame is because *we* did it, *my* generation, and we're leaving it for others to live out.

In my more optimistic moments, I let myself hope a bit. How many possible ends does the world have? Are we really locked into the most catastrophic of all ends? Is it possible that there might still be a down-regulation of the dynamic systems that are popping out of control, like the consumption of fossil fuels or the overproduction of methane? Or the deforestation that destroys the carbon sinks, which release the carbon that traps the planet's heat, which melts the ice caps and decreases the albedo, which leads to more heat absorption, and around and around.

I would sacrifice something to bring about that down-regulation. But how do I make the kind of sacrifice that would be sufficient to delay the end of the world? I can cut down on my own consumption, I can vote for the political parties I judge least likely to do more harm, I can attempt to model minimally hypocritical global citizenship for my students and other young people, and I can donate to organizations that do the heavy lifting of trying to change the political landscape.

But I know these choices are probably too little and too late. In any case, I'm not doing nearly enough, not as much as I could do if I were really committed to putting my weight against the wheel of history. I'm running out of time to accomplish anything helpful, let alone sufficient for ensuring survival—running out of my time, and the world's.

Dalum

I WAS IN THE BADLANDS FOR A FEW DAYS. I drove out of Drumheller one evening to see what I could see, south of the town on Highway 56. The crevasses of the nearly bare hillsides rose up to high fields of canola, topped with sporadic boxy farmhouses and incongruously battered combines and sprayer trucks. I turned west at an intersection called Dalum—a word with no obvious referent anymore, a leftover from early Danish settlers and now indicating nothing but grain and rock and sky. On the secondary highway, I began dropping down and down into valleys carved by what are now shallow streams. I stopped at a place with no name, drawn by the skeletons of old buildings and old cars. A gravel track found on no map led past them to a precarious wooden bridge over the Rosebud River. The track ended on the far side of the bridge, tailing off into scrub and brush as though whoever built it had lost the plot.

The buildings were half-collapsed and of indeterminate age. They were made of weathered grey wood, small-framed (I surmise) because wood is scarce in this part of the province. Each had one opening for a door and several other openings that might have been entrances for goods or vehicles. A line of wooden posts connected by trailing wire ran for a few metres along one of the buildings and then stopped. Someone had jammed upside-down cowboy boots on two of the posts; their leather was split and cracking.

The field of cars was a wonder—rusted American outlines settling almost perceptibly into the ground. It was high summer and the grasses

< Abandoned car found southwest of Drumheller, Alberta. (Photo by the author.)

were tall, flowing over the cars' hoods like a slow-rising tide. Five cars lay within view, pitted with rust and spotted with tiny circles that could have been BB shot or some form of transformation wrought by time and weather. *Why so many vehicles? Who would drive here in the 1930s or 1940s and then just leave the car behind when they decamped? Why were they lined up? Why all pointing in the same direction?* Someone built that bridge, so there must have been a reason to cross the river once. Maybe these cars were relinquished by people coming back, returning from whatever used to be over there. Given the location, an old coal mine was the most likely possibility.

I could feel the slow and purposeless growth of the vegetation, sparse in the dryness, creeping over what remained of vehicles and buildings. I walked out on the bridge and looked between the splintered boards at the Rosebud, seven or eight metres below. It was a tiny river but a fast one, not a meandering creek like the version of the Rosebud I had encountered earlier that day when I took the Road of Eleven Bridges to visit the old hotel in Wayne.

After perhaps forty-five minutes wandering around the bridge and the cars, I turned back towards Drumheller. On a high-summer night the sun stays up until nearly ten o'clock, but I didn't want to risk the dusk, didn't want to be caught out on this highway in the dark, uncertain whether my small headlights would see me home.

Orphans

THE RUINS OF THE WEST are not like the ones I have encountered elsewhere in North America, mainly on the Eastern Seaboard and in the Great Lakes region, where I spent much of my life before moving to Alberta.

I lived in Philadelphia in the 1990s, which at the time was floridly apocalyptic with miles upon miles of abandoned industrial precincts overgrown with vines, and boarded-up rowhouses lining the tracks of the SEPTA commuter train. The water in the city's concrete-channelled canals looked like it hadn't moved since the 1940s. Yet the inhabited neighbourhoods of Philly could be vibrant and vital, and in my own neighbourhood, commerce, recreation, schools, and playgrounds coexisted with decay.

West of Philadelphia, I've passed through the burned-out cities of the depressed US Rust Belt. I can even claim to be from there—the city where I was born, Worcester, Massachusetts, has been called the eastern extreme of the Belt. My father's father worked for US Steel. The abandoned futures of these places are right up in your face; you can walk down any street and there's the chained-off factory, the shell of a house. That kind of ruin is ingrained in American pop culture by now—Bruce Springsteen and Eminem both made their early fortunes from writing and singing about it. Venture farther west beyond the Rust Belt and you'll find more examples. First, you'll get to the Midwest, home of prairie gothic and *In Cold Blood*, and then you'll get to Las Vegas and then to California, the west of which there is no wester, where Nathaniel Hawthorne, Joan Didion, and *Blade Runner* locate their decaying worlds.

The ruins of unrealized futures in the Canadian west are different from those in the east, and also different from those in the American west. Perhaps because there's so much space and so few people, they're spread out thinly and can disappear easily into the background of endless prairie or forest or badlands. In addition, the resource booms that have animated the Canadian west have worked against the preservation of an extensive built record of the past. Edmonton, my home, is a young city that keeps tearing down anything that shows a sign of getting old, and other western cities like Saskatoon and Calgary are similar. But away from the cities, on the long gridded stretches of range roads (north–south) and township roads (east–west), things are different.

Some of the ruins are testimonies to what happens when an economy is dependent on resource extraction, which almost never ends well. Alberta is dotted with old coal mines that boomed and went bust by the 1930s. Sometimes the full external apparatus of the coal mine is still visible, other times there's only an indentation in a hillside or a rotting wooden crossbar to show where men tried to dig out the cheapest, lowest-quality coal. The eastern end of Edmonton's North Saskatchewan River valley is pockmarked with tiny former mines, too many to count, as is the valley of the Red Deer River.

The southern part of Alberta is becoming littered with the traces of another disappearing future, in the form of "orphan wells": oil and gas wells that are no longer producing, but have not been decommissioned by the companies that set them up. The gently nodding pumpjack in the field has become so familiar to me that I don't really register seeing them anymore, but the image of the pumpjack that has stilled, that hasn't moved in who knows how long, registers strongly in my consciousness now as part of the wreckage of oil and gas extraction.

There are somewhere north of fifty thousand orphan wells, sometimes politely referred to as "legacy" wells, in the province. Most have long since gone dry, but still leak contaminants into the soil. Maps of orphan or legacy wells look like a galaxy superimposed on Alberta, with countless dots spiralling out around Drumheller and Crowsnest Pass.

Many orphan wells occupy the same territory that the coal companies opened up in the early twentieth century, and then abandoned when demand for coal fell off as cheaper energy sources, like oil and natural gas, took over in the 1950s. The old coal towns are still there, with a few inhabited houses but not much in the way of commerce, shopping, or educational facilities. East Coulee, Blairmore, Luscar, Anthracite, Coalhurst, Coalspur, Coaldale—once there was no more coal to ship, and no more railroads to ship it on, the towns dwindled. The extraction of natural gas was much less labour-intensive than coal mining and didn't require railroads to move the stuff to market.

The old mining towns are strung like vertebrae along the spines of the old rail lines, on which no trains have run for decades. In places like the Rosebud River valley, the tracks themselves have long since been torn up and carted away, leaving indentations in the land like harrow-marks, and the pilings of bridges that connect nowhere to nowhere else. These are the outlines of the bones left behind when an economic nervous system dies.

Walking around the ruins of the west, especially the ones in rural areas, is an unnerving experience, because there's no way to know whether a former townsite is really, completely, abandoned or whether a few people (eccentrics? hermits?) are still hanging on. *Is that an empty house, or just one that's in need of repair? Does anybody drive their vehicles into that yard of old cars anymore, or has the gate been locked since the 1980s?* How obvious am I, a stranger, poking around the old gas station, taking a picture of the spur line silhouetted against a sunset? And is there anyone left for my presence to offend, anyone who might take issue with my presumption that the history, or the future, of this place is over?

REPUBLIC OF ST. PAUL
(STARGATE ALPHA)

THE AREA UNDER THE WORLDS FIRST
U.F.O. LANDING PAD WAS DESIGNATED
INTERNATIONAL BY THE TOWN OF ST. PAUL
AS A SYMBOL OF OUR FAITH THAT MANKIND
WILL MAINTAIN THE OUTER UNIVERSE FREE
FROM NATIONAL WARS AND STRIFE. THAT
FUTURE TRAVEL IN SPACE WILL BE SAFE FOR
ALL INTER GALACTIC BEINGS. ALL VISITORS
FROM EARTH OR OTHERWISE ARE WELCOME TO
THIS TERRITORY AND TO THE TOWN OF ST. PAUL

St. Paul

STAR TREK is my first memory of the future. My parents were opposed to TV for much of my early childhood, but around my ninth birthday they gave in and acquired a boxy, greyish, mid-1970s black-and-white television, which was even then a bit of an anachronism as most of my school friends had colour sets.

The best thing on TV was *Star Trek*, in the form of reruns of the original series that first aired several months after my birth. I watched all the episodes and memorized vast swathes of dialogue, and for my birthday asked for the paperback retellings of those same episodes. *Star Trek* was folklore for the 1970s, fables and stories that moved from visual to oral to written forms, helped along by the first and possibly the mightiest of all screen-age fandoms. The original series was set in the twenty-third century, which for a nine-year-old seemed as far away as Babylonian or biblical times, but now seems much closer. My great-grandchildren, if there are any, may actually be around when the twenty-third century happens.

It always began with William Shatner intoning, "Space: the final frontier." Frontiers and space and the future fused together in the kinetic images of the title sequence: points of light rushing towards the viewer with a tiny starship *Enterprise* zipping from the left side of the screen to the right. The *Enterprise* wasn't a workaday ship doing boring things, it was a vessel whose mission was to explore—seeking

< *Plaque near the* UFO *landing pad, built in 1967, in St. Paul, Alberta.*
(*Photo by the author.*)

61

out strange new worlds, new life, new civilizations, boldly going, and so forth.

Even as a bedazzled child, I noticed that the surfaces of all the planets of the final frontier looked the same—dusty, craggy, rock-strewn hills with a few spiky succulents and sagebrush. I learned later that *Star Trek* was filmed on a back lot in Culver City, in Los Angeles County. In other words, the future looked a lot like a nondescript bit of Southern California. This association between the landscapes of the west and the idea of the future was strengthened when my father borrowed a projector and reels of science fiction movies from the public library—some that were old even then, like *Planet of the Apes*, and others more current, like *Close Encounters of the Third Kind*.

My expectations about what it would look like on the day the aliens arrived were crystallized into images of the arid west. When I went through a phase of fascination with UFOs, Roswell, and Area 51 a bit later in childhood, it seemed logical that this, too, all happened in the west, Wyoming and New Mexico and Nevada. Where else would the future be? Where else would the aliens want to land?

While the first episodes of *Star Trek* were filming in California, the people of St. Paul, Alberta, were building a UFO landing pad. This was not the work of a local eccentric or a rural dreamer imagining what might be out there in the sky; it was an official municipal project to commemorate Canada's first century as a nation. A CBC news feature about the landing pad claimed that, in St. Paul in 1967, "anyone without a [centennial] project here isn't 'in.' And the farther out the project, the better."

The raised concrete oval in St. Paul, about the size of ten parking spaces, was a stone welcome mat, an expression of the impulse to goodwill and cooperation that animated the science fiction of the times. The landing pad features a mosaic map of Canada made up of pebbles from each province and territory, with the area surrounding St. Paul marked by a large red circle. Local businesses provided all the resources for building the structure, to a total of $11,000. For a few years after it was built, "space sounds" were piped in through a public address system, in order to add a touch of imagined realism. Beside the stairs leading up to the landing pad proper is a plaque with an inscription that manages to be both naïve and sombre:

> As Mankind stands on the threshold of inter galactic travel, let us
> not forget our failures on Earth...If we fail to conquer disease and
> pestilence on Earth, but instead transmit them to other planets, we
> shall never be welcome. If we fail to travel Earth without destroying
> the environment, how shall we ever travel the universe safely. If we
> cannot develop international goodwill among all men, how shall
> we ever develop inter galactic goodwill among all beings. Lastly, if
> Mankind travels this Earth or universe armed with kindness, toler-
> ance, hope and good spirits, he will always be welcomed.

Nearby is another plaque asserting that the landing site belongs to the entire world community, an expression of a hopeful form of internationalism that has almost entirely faded out of public discourse in the early 2020s.

It's difficult to understand, at a remove of more than fifty years, how serious this project was. *For real? Surely nobody actually thought that extraterrestrial life forms would touch down in northern Alberta?* But then—the Russians were in space, the Americans would soon land on the moon, all sorts of things were happening that had never happened before, out there in the sky. Perhaps it wasn't so far-fetched, in 1967, to think that the obvious next step might be first contact with alien beings.

From this distance, what strikes me as most remarkable about the not-a-joke part of it are the assumptions that the aliens would be friendly, that humans would welcome them, and that we'd all somehow get along. I'm reminded of other, more terrestrial, projects of cross-cultural contact during that period, things like Katimavik and Canada World Youth. The former introduced the youth of Canada to one another, whereas the latter introduced them to the world beyond the nation's borders. These programs were still operating when I was a teenager in the mid-1980s; I applied for both, a child of my times, but was accepted by neither. These were forward-looking projects, preparing Canada's young adults for a future of harmony in diversity. They embodied a more upbeat sense of the future, in the interregnum between the barely disguised paranoia of the height of the Cold War in movies like *The Day The Earth Stood Still* and *Invasion of the Body Snatchers* and the dystopian fears of the early 1980s in movies like *Mad Max* and *Escape From New York*.

Even though the landing pad was created in the spirit of upbeat futurism, there is no indication that anyone seriously expected aliens to arrive in St. Paul. The structure is related to that breed of roadside attractions in rural Alberta consisting of ordinary objects reproduced at enormous size, or normal-sized objects displayed in incongruous but prominent places—the world's biggest fishing lure, mushroom, mallard duck, kielbasa sausage, Easter egg, perogy, all lying east of Edmonton, or the front end of an eighteen-wheeler hoisted up into the sky beside a construction pit in the Gwynne valley. Most of these items are in the centre of a small town, usually on a stretch of the main drag that's also a numbered highway, so travellers don't even need to detour in order to snap a quick photo of the largest whatever.

On the day the landing pad was opened in 1967, according to news accounts, the minister of national defence cut the ribbon. Officials from the town paraded to the site dressed as the Martians of the popular imagination, with green skin and bobbing antennae, while go-go dancers in similar getups entertained the crowd. A flying saucer landed in a puff of smoke. Reading about the day's events several decades later, I can't tell how much of this pageantry was legible as kitsch even at the time, how much was straight-up small-town boost-erism, and how much might have been in earnest.

The oval of the landing pad is cracked now, some of the letters have peeled off the signs, and the whole area was overgrown with grass when I visited it a few years ago. The concrete geometry of the architecture hasn't aged that well—if you ignored the mosaic map of Canada, you could be looking at a public facility in Ulaanbaatar, East Berlin, or Chernobyl, bastions of Cold War modernism. The landing pad looks like outdoor recreation equipment for the mega-lithic, brutalist public buildings that had a moment in Alberta cities in the 1960s and 1970s. Buildings like the old art gallery in Edmonton, a four-storey monster that proved impossible to heat adequately and was reconstructed in the early 2000s, the stark façade making way for a swirl of steel and glass to house the art collections. The landing pad and the former art gallery are not ruins, strictly speaking, but they're relics, reminders of futures past.

For a brief period at the end of the millennium, UFOS appear to have had a revival in St. Paul. The town hosted conferences on UFOS in 1998 and 2000, with discussions of crop circles and cattle mutilations, and guests of honour from the world of alien investigation like American physicist Stanton Friedman. A little over a decade later, interviewed for a national newspaper in 2012, the mayor of St. Paul sounded mildly exasperated when he looked back on his predecessor's enthusiasm. "Like it or not, these people in the '60s made that decision and that's what we're known as: the UFO landing pad," he said. "We draw the line at fire hydrants that look like Martians and stuff because we want them to be taken seriously as fire hydrants, right?"

The town also maintained a telephone hotline beginning in 1995 to take calls from people who had spotted UFOS or signs of aliens (1-800-SEE-UFOS). Hundreds of messages were left on the hotline's answering machine before it went dead, at some unknown point in the early 2000s.

I tried to find the transcripts of those calls, wanting to know what motivated people to call a hotline for unearthly encounters, but that information seems to be lost. I'm imagining the callers, from Florida or Brazil or Poland, who saw something in the sky that they couldn't explain, who feared or hoped it might be aliens, reaching for the receivers of landlines or clunky first-generation mobile phones and calling a small town in western Canada. They poured out their information, never receiving a reply, never knowing what would come of it. Someone was listening to their calls, but no one ever picked up the phone.

My Seventies

THE OLDER YOU GET, the more time you've lived through, and by time I mean eras, not just individual years piling up. I read recently that the distance between 2022 and 1980 is the same as the distance between 1980 and 1938—and 1938 was before there was a Second World War, before there was a Cold War, before there was a nuclear era. It doesn't seem possible that when I was in grade ten, I was as far away from 2022 as I was from the 1930s. It doesn't seem possible that my 1970s were closer to the Dirty Thirties than they are to today.

Of all my decades, the 1970s feel the most like home. I don't mean all of the 1970s, of course. I mean the early years, and I mean specifically that part of the 1970s that blew in on the tailwinds of the late 1960s, and I mean the hippies. I am not speaking from direct experience. I was barely sentient during the period of the Summer of Love and Woodstock and the height of Haight-Ashbury. But I was old enough by the mid-1970s to be shaped by the cultural shifts that the 1960s brought about, albeit watered-down and somewhat cleaned up.

We had a *Whole Earth Catalog* at home, and for a while my parents subscribed to *Mother Earth News*. At the summer camp I attended, we sang songs from *Godspell* and *Hair*, and when I was on staff, we used *The New Games Book*, which outlined cooperative games you could play outdoors that had no winners or losers. We were the kids who came along just after these artifacts peaked in North American popular culture. I'm reminded of the Victoria Williams song "Summer of Drugs," about the younger siblings of the hippies, who grew into adolescence in the sunset of all the love and peace, after the good times were over. That described my seventies too.

I know that not all my older siblings (my cultural rather than biological siblings, that is—I'm an oldest child) were hippies. Some of them were early punks, who reacted against the performative sweetness and naturalism of the 1970s by embracing artifice, shock, and aggression. Rebecca Solnit, who's just five years older than me, wrote an essay along these lines. It begins with the quintessential 1970s handicraft—the macramé plant hanger, pendulous and fuzzy—and segues into images of machetes wielded by punks, chopping all that stuff down. Solnit's title, "Rattlesnake in Mailbox: Cults, Creeps, California in the 1970s" tells you everything you need to know about what she thought of the era.

The squalor and violence of the 1970s has spawned a small literary industry of memoirs of mayhem. The 1978 massacre at Jonestown, Guyana, where the dream of communal love, interracial harmony, and living close to the land turned into a nightmare of murder-suicides, produced books like Julia Scheeres's *A Thousand Lives* and John Hall's *Gone from the Promised Land*. Hippie utopias that crashed and burned have also received fictional treatment, tame compared with the accounts of what actually happened, in novels such as Lauren Groff's *Arcadia* or Nancy Peacock's *Life Without Water*.

But when I was a young adolescent growing up in the 1970s, unaware of how such dreams could fail, I wanted (and still want, if I'm honest) to be a hippie. Not a peace-and-grooviness caricature with headband and tie-dye, or a doomed, drugged-out partier at Altamont, but one of the hard-working hippies who went back to the land, reinvented their spirituality, and got in touch with nature in an earnest and serious way.

As a teenager in Toronto, I sought out books about the commune movement. These ranged from earnest tomes like 1973's *Getting Back Together*, by Robert Houriet, to lurid young-adult fiction like Lee Kingman's *The Peter Pan Bag* from 1970, which I think was meant to be a cautionary tale but had quite the opposite effect. I also started rummaging around in the remaining head shops (as they were quaintly called) on Yonge Street, which had windows full of cannabis-related paraphernalia and a few wicker baskets of Indian-cotton clothing in the back, all redolent of sandalwood. On weekend mornings when

my friends and I had nothing better to do than hang around downtown, I would head for Morningstar Imports to dredge the sale bins
in search of a fringed scarf or tiered skirt while my friends went off to
Hercules, the military surplus liquidator, to look for olive-drab pants
that could be pegged in tight or khaki greatcoats, in the style of British
New Wave.

At university I had a different group of friends, more attuned to
what we still called "the counterculture." We were all living away from
our parents for the first time, and our guides for how to make good food
were *Laurel's Kitchen* and the original *Moosewood Cookbook*, first published
in 1976 and 1974 respectively, a decade before our time. I even knew
fellow students who went to the Rainbow Family Gatherings, the perennial paisley-and-psychedelia travelling fairs, although that seemed
pretty frivolous to me.

The alternate-timeline hippie idea of myself was well defined. She
was someone who had put the distractions and materialism of the
North American middle class behind her and had moved to a farm in
Vermont, or New Mexico—or even closer to home, like the area around
Lake Simcoe, a couple of hours north of Toronto, where I'd heard there
was a Christian back-to-the-land experiment. (Later confirmed: it was
called Midian Farm and flourished between 1971 and 1977, according to
a 2018 documentary of the same name. The filmmaker, who was a
child there, is almost exactly my age.)

I imagined getting up early to start the bread in a big stoneware
bowl, hoeing rows of beans, and practising bentwood furniture-making
techniques from *The Foxfire Book*. I would not need much, in this alternate life: work clothes, a couple of warm sweaters, hiking boots. There
would be other people around (even in my daydreams, I knew that
organic farming was too labour-intensive to undertake on my own),
but they would be people like me—people who wanted to live with the
earth and not to harm it, who wanted to make and grow rather than to
shop and consume. In the evening, we would sing bluegrass gospel
tunes. I would never wear makeup again.

It's almost irresistibly easy to make fun of this. Cynicism now comes
to me more quickly than optimism, and I've become very familiar with

the narrative arc of idealism, naïveté, hard reality, and disillusionment. I also know that, while I would probably have been quite useful on a rural commune, I am not cut out for communal living and being so interdependent with so many other people would have driven me mad in short order. And I suspect I vastly discounted the amount of work involved in getting food out of the ground. Even so, the idea of stepping out of an unsatisfying urban life, of volunteering for simplicity and paring your life down to a self-sufficient secular monasticism within a community of like-minded retreatants, *that* idea still drew me.

These daydreams weren't all sweetness-and-light fantasias. They also had an end-times flavour. Somewhere in the back of my mind lay the possibility that I might need self-reliance skills someday, that some as-yet-unspecified apocalyptic thing might happen, and I would have to walk off the grid and begin again. Omar Al-Akkad, in his dystopian novel *American War*, opens with the observation that age cohorts are often identified with the thing that might have destroyed them—so we have the Great War generation, the Great Depression cohort, the AIDS generation, and so forth. My cohort, the early Generation X group, is the end-of-the-world generation, as are probably all the cohorts that come after us. But our Gen-X end of the world was different from the current projections of the end times coming at us through environmental catastrophe.

My generation has always known that civilization might collapse, although back when I was imagining living off the land with friends, the catastrophe that I was expecting was nuclear war. The appeal of being a hippie, of dipping one's own candles and making one's own bread, was fused with the anticipation of a future in which the nuclear plume had risen on the horizon and the radio stations had fallen silent. The science fiction novels I devoured provided plenty of support for such visions. Sometimes the post-civilization worlds they described were off-putting (the clone farms of *Where Late the Sweet Birds Sang*, the religious fanaticism of *The Chrysalids*), and sometimes they were idyllic (the storytelling artists of *Always Coming Home*, the thoughtful pastoralists of *The Wild Shore*). No matter what visions they conjured, they provided fodder for the idea that surviving nuclear war possible, that smaller groups without planet-killing technologies might arise from the ashes.

When I tried to picture what it would be like after I survived the bomb (and I assumed that I would survive; as an adolescent I could not imagine a world without me in it), I envisioned living in a small, decentralized, de-technologized community. That was my best-case scenario. And my real-life touchstone for such a community, my evidence that this might really be possible, lay in my share of a North American collective memory of the hippies, refracted through the beginnings of nostalgia in the decade or two after it all happened.

| The 1970s introduced me to pastoral utopias and their obverse, nuclear apocalypticism. But the reason the 1970s are my decade is because that's when I learned to read and write. Almost everyone learns these skills as a child, but for some of us, words become something pretty close to life itself.

As a child in the seventies, I read and read and read in a way that was probably only possible for those few generations born after the proliferation of libraries and cheap paperbacks, but before the rise of entertainment on screens. When well-meaning adults who had observed that I liked reading asked "What are you reading now?" or "What kinds of books do you like?" I goggled blankly at them in an unhelpful way. Where would I start? Where does one begin to describe the world?

Along with being a voracious reader, I've always known myself to be "a good writer," which is different from knowing yourself to be a writer, full stop. A good writer is a person who is good at writing, who is comfortable with words and sentences and making sense, whereas a writer, *tout court*, to me at least, is someone for whom writing is not just something you do but the only thing you do, the only thing that matters.

A writer (or a *real* writer) meant someone with a bone-deep commitment to writing that I couldn't find in myself. I think of Emily Dickinson, sequestered in her room, communing with the world by pen and paper, or Simone de Beauvoir, centring her life and politics on her writing work in the cafés of Paris. Or, less appealing, I think of the wild male authors of the great white canon: Ernest Hemingway and Norman Mailer and Dylan Thomas and Ted Hughes and Raymond Carver and Andre Dubus, possessed with a need to write that is represented as being almost uncontrollable, and existing in self-destroying symbiosis with other passions, namely alcohol or danger or extreme beliefs. I might be good at writing, but I don't have it at the core of my being, and so for years I didn't think that whatever talent I might have was adequate for a life spent with literature as my daimon.

Nonetheless, by the end of the seventies, I had begun to think that I ought to be writing words down, as well as consuming them. Had it been twenty years later, I might have started a blog on LiveJournal or WordPress; thirty or forty years later, I might have launched into social media. It's probably a good thing that, at the time, only the private world of ink and paper was available to me.

For Christmas when I was thirteen, my parents gave me a notebook from a shop in Chinatown. It had a sort of upholstered cover embroidered with metallic red threads, and lined pages of a friable texture I had never encountered before. I headed the first page *December 25, 1979*, and began to write what I thought a diary entry ought to be, based on Anne Frank and Harriet the Spy. I got about two-thirds of the way down the page describing my Sunday school teacher and the slippers I also received as a Christmas present.

Then I stalled out. I couldn't think of what to write next, and I was excruciatingly, exquisitely aware of how contrived this all was. *Here I am, pretending to be a girl who keeps a diary, putting this on for the benefit of no one.* Was I trying to fool myself? I was a reader, not a writer. I had no idea what to say, and festered in an obscure resentment of the idea that I *ought* to have something to say.

I found things to say eventually. That notebook yielded accounts of the complex social dynamics of an almost incestuously close-knit group of school friends, in which every interaction was given outsized opinion and described in ethnographic detail. Certainly there was a lot of misery in these observations; I was not inclined to tell my diary · about feeling happy and blithe, and there wasn't much to be happy about either. Friends who "knew me when" tell me that I was just fine during those years, perhaps a bit spacey and nerdy, but also smart and funny. Of course, I was not conscious of that social version of myself, so she never appears in that notebook's early pages.

Because I was a middle-class white girl growing up in the 1970s and 1980s, the person I most wanted to emulate was Sylvia Plath, whose collected journals I read over and over until the yellow-and-brown paperback began to disintegrate. I was certain that I harboured thoughts as complex and profound as hers. I just needed to be sure I wrote them down before they vanished into ephemerality. So I started to write more frequently, trying to aestheticize the palace intrigues of high school and young adulthood rather than just record them.

The results were mixed. I did keep journals more or less regularly, until I was into my mid-thirties. I always had a notebook of some sort with me, and frequently had the intention of writing in it. I had a vague sense that I should be writing more often, because I had things to say (*to whom?*), but this did not translate into a passion. I had a notebook always with me, but the need to write, the inner fire, was never as strong as I half-wanted it to be.

In my memory, the journal entries are scattered thinly across those years, each at a great remove from the others. But when I revisit the notebooks, their remarkable number tells a different story. I wrote much more frequently than I thought I did. The vague sense that I should be writing more didn't match the reality, which was that I actually did chronicle my life pretty faithfully. I had a tendency to write more when in the grip of a depressive episode, trying to figure it out and work it through. Looking back, I wonder, *Was I really that unhappy, that much of the time?* The answer, I am afraid, is yes.

I'm reading Sharon Butala's *This Strange Visible Air*, in which she reflects on her life as a writer and a person growing older. Butala remembers the tangle of emotions she felt on being nominated for the Governor General's Award for a short story collection, and convincing herself that it would be fine if she did not win, that the nomination should be enough, that getting this recognition for her writing was not that important, that she was not one of those monsters of desire who want too much fame and recognition. That she could put the whole enterprise of being a writer to the side if she wanted.

But then, Butala writes:

> I was alone in my office in the luminous shadows just before night fell and an axe came down from above and split me open from the top of my skull to my pubic bone. With this bloodless painless vision came the knowledge that I was a liar. That I would always put my writing ahead of any other significance demand on me and that there was nothing and nobody for whom I would stop.

I can't live up to that axe, that sunset reckoning, that blaze of certainty. I never imagined that there was nothing and nobody for whom I would stop writing—indeed, most of the time there seemed to be nothing for which I would *start* writing, even when I knew I had something to say, even when I could feel the words pulling at me. Especially once I became an adult, I had a sense of a shadow standing between me and the blank page, and whatever pull I felt towards putting my life into words was seldom enough to push the shadow aside and write about myself.

So I wrote about a lot of other things, mainly work. The work of my adult life has been as a professor in a publish-or-perish world, in which I did very well thanks to my ability to write to publication, to adapt tone and register and vocabulary to suit a specialized academic journal, or a newspaper's opinion column. And I had a second piece of good writing fortune, in that I never got writer's block. I might not burn with the blazing heat and light of more passionate writers, but I also never experienced the sudden drying-up, the descent of blankness. I could almost always produce something serviceable, on time and on point.

Coming back to the life-writing of adolescence took a very long time. I had to go through a series of crises, events that were earth-shaking to live through but really not that uncommon, and come out the other side. I had to think of myself as someone who had made a decent life for herself. I had to have a place of security to write from.

In the past three or four years, writing about myself started to feel right. It felt like the unfurling of a phantom limb, or perhaps some sort of wing, some part of me that had been quiescent for almost too long. Most of what I wrote was terrible—but by this point I'd had plenty of experience with things that started out terribly and gradually got better. I was confident that, with the fullness of time, the amount of good writing would exceed the bad. Twenty years ago, I might not have been so confident and would have given up after the first extended streak of terrible writing. This is another reason why I could not have returned to personal writing any sooner than I actually did.

And here I am today. I suppose I am a writer. But I am still not entirely certain that I merit the designation. I am a reasonably good artisan with words, not an inspired artist. Yet something keeps me going with the pen and the page and the laptop screen, beyond mere competence. Whatever that something is, it first began growing inside me in very early youth, in the seventies, when nothing was more vivid or more important than words on a page.

Strathcona Science Park

EDMONTON CONSTANTLY REBUILDS ITSELF. In this respect, it is similar to other midwestern and western oil towns. I recall visiting Oklahoma City a couple of decades ago, marvelling at the long low spaces and the way the oldest buildings looked to be younger than I was, as though someone had invented a city sometime around 1980.

Likewise, Edmonton does not have many architectural shadows of its past, as very little built space is allowed to crumble or decay. In Philadelphia, where I lived in the late 1990s before moving to Edmonton, I could walk for hours through blocks of abandoned buildings and empty parks, and read three centuries of the city's history off the façades of what was left behind, the old warehouses and schools and churches. Edmonton doesn't have that kind of legible cityscape, but it does have the Strathcona Science Park.

The science park has nothing to do with science anymore. It's officially a provincial park, but ecologically and geographically it's part of the system of city parks that runs along both sides of the North Saskatchewan River. The science park is at the eastern edge of the city limits, bordered by Strathcona County's oil refineries and the businesses that serve them. There's a privately run ski hill to the north, and to the south, a pitted road leads to a traffic artery eastbound to Sherwood Park, once the bedroom suburb of the refineries.

< *Sign signalling the miniature airfield at Strathcona Science Provincial Park, in Edmonton, Alberta.* (Photo by author.)

Nothing about the park is obvious. A discreet sign announces that you're entering Strathcona Science Provincial Park as you turn off 17 Street by some refinery storage tanks and clank over the railway tracks. The first time I saw the sign, I was driving around randomly and my attention was caught by the portmanteau nature of the name. *What's a "science" provincial park?*

Following the turnoff didn't provide me with any clues at first. There isn't much to see, except for an overly large and oddly placed parking area on a plateau overlooking the river valley. The rest of the riverbank is wooded with stands of poplar and thickets of dogwood, so this open space seems not to be part of its surroundings. It looks like it belongs farther south, perhaps down around Calgary, where grasslands or former grasslands dominate the terrain.

Walk across the parking lot towards the river, and you'll find what remains of the science park from the days when it was in its prime. There's an octagonal brick building, about the size of a gas station, with boarded-up doors and straggly grass growing out of cracks in the concrete. There are a few informational signs, beige metal with text in that distinctive sans-serif font that I associate with Canadian public education efforts of the 1970s, the last optimistic decade before political and economic life began to contract under conservative austerity governments in the 1980s. I have a lapel pin from Parks Canada with that same font and earth-toned colour scheme, yellow words below a stylized brown beaver.

The signs inform me that there used to be small-scale coal mines scattered along the riverbanks. These are long since collapsed and deserted. One sign says that a brick chimney remains from the biggest of the mines, but it's not evident. Scrambling around the hillside, I spot a couple of indentations that might have been the entrances to small mines, no bigger than a man could crawl into, now overgrown with tangles of red osier dogwood.

Other informational signs near the parking lot tell me that this is a significant archaeological site, and that the archaeology laboratory on the premises holds the evidence of thousands of years of human habitation. This would put the science park area on a par with the Rossdale flats a few kilometres up the river. Only there is no archaeological laboratory here anymore, at least none that I can find. There are a few wood-framed sets of stairs along the riverbank that lead nowhere, and a few crumbling concrete pads.

Perched on the cliff overlooking the river, with the silhouettes of downtown buildings off to the west and nobody else around, the setting evokes *The Twilight Zone*—which, in my memory, relied heavily on images of empty spaces or places where human activity used to be in order to suggest the uncanny. The near-monochrome palette in every direction—beige and grey foliage, grey river, brown buildings, silver-grey refinery stacks—also calls up the old TV set from my childhood, on which all possible futures appeared in black and white.

The science park opened in 1980, just over a decade after the bigger and more elaborate Ontario Science Centre opened near Toronto. It was a modernity project, promising a future of high technology and sleek engineering for a blue-collar city like Edmonton, reflected in its futuristic architecture. Old drawings of the park's layout show a network of windowless octagonal pods, looking as though they had just landed on Earth, connected by concrete walkways at odd angles, with lines of tall pylons marching off into the distance. You could be forgiven for thinking of *Planet of the Apes*, or the campus of the University of California, Irvine, where one of the *Apes* movies was filmed.

The science park was built by a provincial government that was flush with oil and gas revenue in the 1970s. It was meant to anchor the eastern perimeter of the city, and have its own bus line and recreation area (which survives as the ski hill). It's one of a group of Edmonton infrastructure projects from the 1960s and 1970s that are just slightly less impressive than their Toronto analogs—the original Royal Alberta Museum (based on the Royal Ontario), the city's CN Tower (so much shorter than the Toronto version, which was in its day the tallest free-standing object in the world), and even the Edmonton "subway," the light rail transit line that cuts an odd diagonal across the city, with stops where there seems to be no reason for an LRT stop to be. As an Albertan, I find these things faintly embarrassing, as though elected officials forty or fifty years ago were all too visibly determined to prove to the world that western cities could compete with anything in central Canada, the national centre of gravity.

The Strathcona Science Park functioned as intended for less than a decade. After eight years, it was closed when oil prices plunged, as they do at least once a decade. Of the six educational pavilions that made up the park, only the one graffitied octagon remains. When I first explored the site, it had been abandoned for almost four times as long as it was inhabited. After the science park was closed, city staff discovered that the land on which it was built was contaminated. Decades of coal mining and dumping waste over the bluffs of the river had filled the soil with toxins. Nothing new can be built there now.

Last winter when I returned to the park's trails for a walk, I encountered a middle-aged man with his teenage son at the edge of the parking lot, looking lost and slightly frustrated. "This is the science centre, yes?" said the man, holding up his phone on which Google Maps was open. "Are there things we can see?" I imagined him as a harried but engaged parent, trying to get his son moving, on an outing to somewhere wholesome with educational value. Unfortunately, there was nothing there for them. I said no, it's been gone for a long time.

I turned towards the river and went down a level to a slightly lower plateau. A few signs, battered and somewhat crooked, had been planted among the grass. They warned me to beware of remote-controlled aircraft overhead, and to not trespass on the takeoff and landing zone. *Trespass on what? A lot of quackgrass? What aircraft?*

So of course I did trespass, and followed a faint trail of bent-over stems to what gradually revealed itself as a tiny, deserted micro-airport. It was the headquarters of the Strathcona Remote Control Flyers Association: a miniature runway, a few benches, a boxed-in area where I assume the remote aircraft handlers waited their turn to launch their planes. There was an empty noticeboard and a commemorative plaque on one of the benches for someone called Metro Kondriuk, bearing the date 2008. Past the benches and a small parking lot, the refineries of Sherwood Park smoked and flared on the horizon.

The tiny airfield looked like it had been around since the heyday of the science park. Even the phrasing was a bit antique—"remote flyers" are what we would probably call drone pilots today. Despite the caution signs and warnings of danger, I could see no one to whom those admonitions might apply, no wanderers who might interrupt a flight, no remote pilots with their controls and their tiny craft. The airfield looked half-inhabited, like the science park—not yet entirely vanished, but not entirely present either.

The Years Before Me, the Years Behind

I HAVE MORE YEARS BEHIND ME than in front of me, so in a mathematical sense my time is running out. When I try to picture time running out, I imagine a wall clock ticking steadily towards midnight, like a 1950s version of the memento mori hourglass in Renaissance paintings. When I try to contemplate that wall clock, try to picture the mechanisms of the timepiece, I think, *Well, that clock's never kept very good time anyway. It's always been a bit fast or a bit slow.* So have I.

I've done things, major life things, not always at the right time or at least not at the time that was typical of my peers, middle-class Gen-Xers now in their mid-fifties. I finished high school and university a couple of years early, while still in my late teens, and got married relatively early too, when I was twenty-three, to someone I had been with for five years already. I delayed having a baby for the reasons common to my cohort—post-secondary education, and then post-post-secondary education, and then the establishment of a career. But instead of taking five or six years to start a family, I waited until I was thirty-nine.

I was an *elderly primigravida*, to use the archaic and obnoxious term for a woman who gets pregnant for the first time when well into adulthood, a term that was still current in Alberta medical records back then.

I believe this was the first time the word *elderly* was ever applied to me in any context.

My elderly primigravida status meant that I was classified as a "high-risk pregnancy," according to medical definitions at the time. So I had my checkups in a high-risk OB-GYN's office, whose patients consisted mainly of other pregnant people who were out of time. On one side of the waiting room, you had the late-thirties and early-forties group, most of whom were either studiously reading and highlighting *What to Expect When You're Expecting*, or looking exasperated and bored by what I imagined to be an unexpected perimenopausal pregnancy. On the other side, you had very young teenagers with Big Gulps and early smartphones on which they texted non-stop, and often with mothers of their own in tow. Until I became visibly pregnant, it might not have been clear to an observer whether I was in the waiting room as someone who would soon give birth, or as a grandmother-to-be. (I understand that the province's upper age cut-off for a high-risk pregnancy has now been moved upwards, from thirty-five to forty, reflecting changes in the trajectories of Albertans' reproductive lives.)

During my daughter's toddler years, I was mistaken more than once for her grandmother, especially once my hair started to go grey in my mid-forties. The person making the mistake was always anxiously apologetic once they figured out that the child was my own progeny, as though they had accused me of perpetrating some sort of fraud and were concerned that I should not think less of them for their error.

One young father at a playground in northeast Edmonton apologized effusively after he told his tiny son to "ask the little girl's grandma" if the boy could play with one of my daughter's sand toys. One apology wasn't enough, however, and he came over to my bench a second time to explain that he'd taken me for a grandmother because I looked like his mother-in-law, who was "really young and athletic." For reasons that are still not entirely clear to me, I made a show of scrambling to the top of the climbing wall while laughing and interacting with my daughter, as though I needed to validate the young father's explanation for his mistake through a display of youthful athleticism.

At the time of the incident I wondered, *Why does he sound so stricken? Why does he presume it would be a terrible thing to be a woman who looks older than she really is?* These questions are informed by a feminist sensibility that rejects the assumption that the best thing a woman can be is young and conventionally pretty. Now, as I look back on that day, my questions have changed a bit. Now I ask myself, *Why did I need to set him straight? Why did I feel the need to fit myself into the correct generational order of things, asserting that I was a mother and not a grandmother? Why was it important to disavow the status of an older woman?*

I seemed to hit the life-course milestones that index age, like marriage and parenthood, at odd times. I was early to marry and late to procreate, but early again to end the marriage (early, that is, in terms of years I had lived, not in terms of the length of the marriage). Before I got divorced, I had only one friend who had ended her marriage. Her divorce, when I first heard about it, was both awe-inspiring and apocalyptic in its newness. My divorce, the story of which I won't tell here, meant that I was only the second person in my peer group to enter that particular terrain of last things. But since then, the pace of divorces around me has quickened. The people I know are splitting up one after another, as if I had set off an invisible row of dominoes with the end of my own marriage.

By now, more than half of my friends have at least one finished marriage or long-term relationship behind them. The length of my first marriage—twenty-five years—is no longer remarkable, as unions of thirty or thirty-five years or more are coming to their ends. (I seem to have some sort of social filter that selected for people who stay with partners for a long time, whether or not the union was ill-starred from the beginning, and so most of the endings I hear about are of couplings that lasted for decades.)

Although I don't wish the sadness and toxicity and anger of even the most civilized divorce on anyone, there's a bit of comfort in having arrived at a stage in life in which I'm no longer a pioneer. Many of my daughter's friends have divorced parents, and I am no longer subject to the assumption—by teachers, coaches, neighbours, and other third parties—that I am married to, or otherwise have contact with, the other parent of my child. The clock has ticked on long enough that, in a roomful of parents my age, I'm no longer out in front when it comes to the end of marriages and long-term partnerships and the embarkation on solo or post-divorce shared parenting. Of the parents I know now, close to half of them have ended a marital or domestic relationship with the person with whom they used to co-parent. In this respect, I've caught up with the clock, or it has caught up with me.

Other parts of my life, beyond the big-ticket items of marriage and parenting, also seem to be catching up with the clock. Physical embodiment—running, biking, hiking, and doing it all voluntarily—has become a much bigger part of my life than it was in my younger years. I never considered myself an athlete when I was younger and arguably more suited for pushing my physical limits, but I started running in the spring of 2018, when I was fifty-two. I began because a work friend had invited and/or challenged a group of colleagues to a road race in the mountains in the fall, and I hoped rather desperately to be able to get through five kilometres without dying or embarrassing myself. As it happened, I found that I loved running even more than five kilometres' worth. I ran my first (and so far, only) ten kilometres in Banff that fall, placing in the exact middle of my age group. We had plans to race again in 2019, but a freak snowstorm derailed us, and then came 2020 and everybody knows what that meant.

My style of running, insofar as I had one, was pretty anarchic and undisciplined. It consisted of lacing up running shoes, tucking my keys somewhere, and taking off in no particular direction for as long as I could go. I say "had" and "was" because I stopped running in early 2020.

I had to stop running because of another anarchic and undisciplined activity—tobogganing down an icy hill with big trees at the bottom and slamming into one such tree, hitting just below my right kneecap. I was out on the hill with my fourteen-year-old daughter and one of her oldest friends, who had been zipping down over and over without incident, and I decided it looked like fun.

It was not fun. The outcome was a complete severing of the right posterior cruciate ligament, or PCL. For months and then years afterwards, my proprioception and balance were distorted, and my shin appeared to have moved back a few centimetres behind my right knee. Whenever I tried running, a cord of pain would wrap around my leg where the lost ligament used to be. And I would remember the sports doctor's strong advice, which was not to push my luck and make it worse. Pain meant stop.

So I became a walker. At first I didn't think much about walking, except as an inferior form of running, until the pandemic happened and walking became what I did, all the time, every day. Pre-pandemic, walking had been how I got from one place to another, as a healthier and often more interesting alternative to other forms of locomotion. With the pandemic, the walking became an end in itself, because there was nowhere really to go. I had a Fitbit and an app on my phone to track my steps and distances, but using them was just rote quantification, a habit of self-monitoring. I counted my kilometres, but that wasn't the point.

Over the past few years, walking has also become a little universe, a self-contained sphere of sensation. When I head out the door, I anticipate a shift in my perceptions and preoccupations, just as I did in my running days. However, instead of the exhilaration and endorphins of a good hard run, I move sideways into a parallel world, in which the fret and worry of daily life dims to a background blur.

It's got something to do with the oscillation between left and right, activating one side and then the other, constant motion and constant rhythm. I've read about the virtues of bilateral stimulation, whether it be drumming or tapping or dance, and the trance-like state it can induce. From left side to right side and again and again—I experience a slow and reliable recalibration. I walk around the neighbourhood or down into the river valley and out again, waiting for a pleasant physical fatigue to seep into me.

When I first started running in 2018, I wanted to be able to finish five or ten kilometres on mountain roads without collapsing, which meant building strength and endurance. Somewhere between then and now, that motivation changed to maintaining whatever strength and endurance I already have. That moment should have been a watershed, the shift from building to sustaining, only I didn't notice when it happened. But yesterday when I was out walking, I began to wonder why I was doing this. The words came into focus unbidden: *So I'll live for a long time, and so I'll have a good death.*

Each fall as Yom Kippur rolls around, I'm reminded of Unetanneh Tokef, the Hebrew prayer for those who will die in the year to come. The prayer lists the ways in which they might go: fire, water, wild beast, sword, and so on. I'm not likely to go in any of those ways. But how *will* I go?

I don't want a bad death. I have now seen enough people much older than me suffering from dementia, incapacitated by strokes, continuing to exist in conditions that I know they would not have chosen for themselves. I can't do much about the unpredictable, but I can try to stave off the conditions that I know are linked to debilitation and decay.

So—I exercise, eat good food, get regular checkups, monitor levels of this and that in my blood. I am getting myself ready for what I hope will be a long life. But it becomes increasingly clear to me that I am also readying myself for a short death.

Newbrook

THE NEWBROOK OBSERVATORY is in the hamlet of the same name. It's just off Highway 63, the road travelled by enormous trucks hauling oilfield equipment to Fort McMurray, three hundred kilometres north. There are only two buildings on the observatory site, both smaller than the average bungalow, neither in use anymore.

The observatory was a fruit of postwar cooperation between Canada and the United States. The site was selected, in part, because Newbrook was far from any source of human-made light that might contaminate the skies, but not so far north that the aurora borealis would interfere with meteor spotting. The Americans wanted to see and track meteors as part of the great expansion in physical sciences after the Second World War, but also because of the concern that the Soviets were using meteor tracking infrastructure to scan for the presence of American satellites. And in this respect, Newbrook delivered.

Constructed in the early 1950s, the Newbrook observatory had its moment of glory in 1957. That was the year the Cold War turned into the space race, as the Soviet Union put the first Sputnik satellite into Earth orbit. Sputnik launched from Baikonur in present-day Kazakhstan, a city that, in the Soviet era, did not officially exist. The Soviets announced to the world that Sputnik was in the sky on October 4, setting off consternation and envy in the United States and allied nations. The first photographic confirmation of this new entity in space came on October 9, from the Newbrook observatory.

< *Intersection in Newbrook, Alberta.* (Photo by the author.)

Newbrook is only a few kilometres from Abee, an even smaller hamlet where a 236-pound stone fell out of the sky on June 9, 1952, at nearly midnight. The fiery trace of the object's path would have been visible across Canada, but the stone itself was only found five days later, by a farmer tending his wheat field. The origins of the iron-rich Abee meteorite are unknown—some speculate that it was part of the surface of Mercury, where it formed four billion years ago, or that it broke off an asteroid body in Mercury's orbit a bit more recently than that.

The jewel of the Newbrook observatory was a device called the Super-Schmidt meteor camera. Only six of these were ever manufactured, and two of them ended up in Alberta: one at Newbrook and the other at the Meanook observatory, about fifty kilometres northwest. The camera was about the size of steamer trunk and was mounted beneath a special retractable roof, made of two sliding panels on rails. When night fell, the panels would be moved apart by the astronomer, and the camera could be manoeuvred into position under the stars.

The Newbrook observatory was (and is) a building about the size of a single-car garage, with an adjoining office and a nearby residence. Arthur Griffin, the first astronomer in residence, could watch the skies from an angled swivel chair under the office's glass roof, a setup he referred to as "the coffin." Griffin's speciality was meteors—finding them, tracking them, confirming their existence. He was recruited straight out of his science degree at the University of Toronto by Peter Millman of the Dominion Observatory, and was dispatched to Alberta with his new bride, Evelyn Treleaven, to tend the Newbrook and Meanook Super-Schmidt cameras. The Griffins were based in Newbrook, closer to the centre of Alberta, and Arthur travelled up north to Meanook as needed.

The only published account of the Griffins' life in Newbrook, by Canadian historian of astronomy Richard Jarrell, describes it as solitary and often monotonous. They lived beside the observatory in a frame house with no insulation or running water for the first few years. They broke long stretches of tedium with trips to the other Super-Schmidt camera at Meanook, or to Edmonton, on roads that consisted of dust, ice, or mud, depending on the season. During the long, long days of the northern summer, the Griffins took vacations, returning to Newbrook and Meanook as the days grew shorter and the opportunity for night work returned.

In the 1950s, astronomy was a labour of the dark. Griffin's work day began around eleven o'clock at night. Working alone or with the staff stationed at Meanook, he would identify sections of the sky to photograph with the Super-Schmidt or smaller, more portable cameras. The cameras had to be carried outdoors, and required twelve-minute exposures at fifteen-minute intervals. When clouds covered the sky, or when the moon was full and bright, the night's work might be cancelled. On dark work nights when the temperature was too cold for Griffin to endure being outside, he fitted himself into the coffin and watched the sky through the glass roof for hours, noting down what he saw.

Griffin's job as a field astronomer in the 1950s meant that he and his family spent their years in small places with abundant darkness, far away from the centres of academic physics and astronomy. The sighting and photographing of Sputnik was a break in the routine of meteor observation, and briefly made Newbrook famous in geopolitical circles. The Soviets had announced that they had put a satellite into Earth orbit, but the distrust and suspicion between the USSR and the United States meant that the American government wanted independent confirmation. Ham radio operators across the continent could track Sputnik by listening to its beeps as it passed far overhead, but Griffin was the first person to take a picture of it. No human-made object had ever been as far away from Earth as the tiny dot that he photographed on an early autumn evening in 1957.

I visited Newbrook in 2017, and again in 2022. There are only four streets to the town, and on my most recent visit, there were no functioning businesses on any of them. The street signs bore whimsical names related to outer space and astronomy: Sputnik Street, Jupiter Avenue, Meteor Street. The block that must have once been the centre of town was silent, lined with boarded-up, single-storey buildings that once housed small retail operations. One building displayed a sign indicating that it was a branch of ATB Financial, a fixture in many rural towns, but it, too, was closed and showed no sign of life.

I parked adjacent to the main street, beside a vacant lot and an RV up on concrete blocks with a for-sale sign. There was no one around, but my presence set off a cascade of barking, passed from one unseen dog to the next, as I walked quickly to the railroad tracks to look for the observatory. I'm not usually prone to getting bad vibes or creepy feelings from places, but Newbrook was an exception. (The histories of the observatory suggest that the town was not always so silent. The Griffins reportedly stayed in a hotel in Newbrook while waiting for their house to be built, and the farmer who found the Abee meteorite brought it to a hardware store in Newbrook to be weighed.)

When I was there in 2022, the only indication of the observatory was a sign pointing down an overgrown path on the edge of the town proper. I could walk right up to the observatory building and residence and look through the dusty windows, most of which were still intact. I noticed a few bits of furniture inside the house—a table, some chairs— and a stack of papers, of what sort I couldn't tell. The observatory itself, with the retractable roof on rails, had an improvised, do-it-yourself look. The paint was chipping. The wooden boards of the roof were uneven and rough, and the rails were rusty and somewhat warped. In late 2020, Thorhild County received a grant from the provincial government to restore the observatory, and the local historical society sourced one of the last remaining Super-Schmidt cameras to be reinstalled under the panels that slide open to the black sky. However, at the time I visited, no restoration was evident.

The slightly unkempt exterior, the scattered objects inside the residence, and the lack of formal signage marking the property as a historic site made it look as though the astronomer and his family had just stepped away—perhaps on their summer vacation, when the hours of sunlight kept darkness out of the sky, and the grass around the home and office grew longer in the family's absence.

Arthur Griffin saw the light that was Sputnik in the sky, but no human hands touched the satellite after it was launched. Sputnik degraded and burned up in Earth's atmosphere after only a few months in orbit. It went from Earth into space and soon disappeared. But other lights in the sky have come down to Earth's surface in Alberta, and some were taken up into human history, given meaning and significance. These objects were not made by human hands, but they reside in human imaginations.

Newbrook is about two hundred and fifty kilometres from Hardisty, Alberta, which was the terrestrial home of the Manitou Stone, known as papâmihâw-asiniy in Plains Cree. This meteorite, 145 kilograms of almost pure iron and 4.5 billion years old, is an object of spiritual focus for the Plains Cree and Blackfoot. In 1866, a Methodist missionary named George McDougall kidnapped the stone. McDougall moved it to a mission in the Victoria Settlement, about a hundred kilometres northeast of Edmonton, in the apparent expectation that the Indigenous people would follow their stone straight to his church, where he could convert them to Christianity. They did not.

The removal of the Manitou Stone occurred at the beginning of a decade of disasters for many First Nations, including a smallpox outbreak and the disappearance of the bison in the region. Ten years after the Manitou Stone was taken, Treaty 6 was signed between the colonial government and the leaders of First Nations across much of what is now central Alberta and Saskatchewan. The First Nations signed under the compulsion of hunger from the disappearance of the bison and the fear of smallpox, agreeing to resettle on demarcated reserves within their own territories in exchange for the provision of medical supplies, a bit of cash, the promise of schools, and protection against other groups of settlers who wanted to take over the fertile river valleys.

The Manitou Stone was later taken even farther: it was moved from McDougall's church to Victoria College at the University of Toronto, which was a centre for missionary training in the late nineteenth and early twentieth centuries. It was not returned to Alberta until 1972, when the University of Toronto sent it to Alberta's provincial museum, where it was displayed among other relics of the "native tribes" of the area.

In 2018, the Royal Alberta Museum moved to a much bigger down-town location. The Manitou Stone now has a gallery of its own, with a sign asking visitors to respect its cultural significance and refrain from taking its picture. It has still not returned to the place from which it was taken, some two hundred kilometres from Edmonton. In the fall of 2022, the provincial government committed to repatriating the stone and to building a prayer centre to house it.

I visited the stone in the museum in 2020. I had imagined the Manitou Stone would be something the size of an old-fashioned travel trunk that could easily fit into a nineteenth-century missionary's horse wagon, but it is much bigger, about the size of Arthur Griffin's "coffin." I walked around and around it, trying to impress on my memory the sight of papâmihâw-asiniy. I thought of the many other stones that cross the Alberta sky, orbiting or falling, and the thousands of pictures taken of them by Arthur Griffin during all the lonely nights at the Newbrook observatory.

Ancestors and Descendants

A FEW YEARS AGO, I heard an interview on CBC Radio with Chelsea Vowel, a Métis scholar who lives on Treaty 6 territory. She was talking about the Cree language, how the same word may be used for both ancestors and descendants. Vowel was discussing her 2022 book *Buffalo Is the New Buffalo*, a collection of what she calls "Métis futurisms," stories that reach simultaneously for the future and the past, unsettling linear notions of time. I was intrigued and sought out her book. I learned from the short story "âniskôhôcikan" that ancestors and descendants can both be called âniskôtapanak. In the story, an Elder explains this concept by describing a string of beads: the beads are attached to one another by the string, but the string itself can be pulled taut, bunched up, twisted back on itself.

I wanted to know more. I looked up Cree–English glossaries and articles about Cree linguistics online. I learned that in Cree, terms for intergenerational kinship are not always stratified by heredity the way they are in the European languages I know, in which the most salient difference between me and my grandparents or grandchildren is whether I preceded them on Earth or they preceded me. For instance, in Plains Cree, according to an online dictionary, nitâniskôhpicikan can mean both a great-grandparent and a great-grandchild, both an ancestor and a descendant.

I am sure that I don't grasp the meaning of the words in their totality because I am a stranger to Cree languages and Cree ways of knowing.

Nonetheless, I was captured by the idea that words of kinship not only index the linearity of relations—who preceded whom—but also the distance (and therefore the connection) between people.

This suggests a way of thinking about time that is similar to the way I think about space: if somewhere or something is a couple of hundred kilometres north, a couple of hundred kilometres south, which place is ahead of me, and which way is behind? It depends on the direction I am facing. And I can change direction; I am not locked into only one form of forward.

My ancestors and my descendants are both far from me in time, but also always present within me. I do not yet know the names of my descendants, and I can only name a few of my ancestors. Yet, as Vowel said, we are always ancestors and descendants ourselves, whether we know our relations or not.

This is an oddly comforting thought as I consider my westbound path. It sets me into an enduring immortal configuration, and it also creates an ethical responsibility to be a good ancestor, because my descendants need me to be that ancestor. My generation, as a group, has poisoned the planet that these descendants will inherit, so the least we can do, the least I can do, is try to be a good progenitor who leaves something of value for them. The obligation to be a good ancestor is a weighty responsibility, but it is also an opportunity to be significant, to know that my life means (or has meant or will mean) something in the cosmos, even if, at times and from my limited perspective, I fear that it didn't mean very much.

Wostok and Spaca Moskalyk

MY PARTNER AND I wanted to get out of Edmonton for a few hours and decided to drive northeast, aiming vaguely for the Vinca Bridge. East of that bridge, if you keep going dead straight on Highway 45, you enter what's known as the Ukrainian heartland of northern Alberta. In the late nineteenth century, this is where settlers began to arrive from Ukraine (or more precisely, from Galicia, Ruthenia, Bukovyna, and the Austro-Hungarian Empire, places that are no longer countries).

The remains of tiny farming hamlets are scattered across the compass-sharp grid of range roads and township roads. Wostok (or Star-Wostok, as it was also known) was part of the Edna-Star colony, the earliest rural ethnic enclave in Alberta. It was settled in 1891 by a group of peasants from what is now Ivano-Frankivsk Oblast in Ukraine, with later arrivals coming from both Ukrainian-speaking and German-speaking regions of Russia.

Many of the families who made the move to Canada had been loggers in the old country, until it became deforested. Descriptions of acres of untouched trees in Canada West pulled them across the ocean, just as descriptions of open grasslands to the south and the east pulled other European settlers. Their first homes were made of sod, some barely more than dugouts. These dwellings subsided back

< *Abandoned buildings in Wostok, Alberta.* (Photo by the author.)

into the earth that birthed them within a few decades. The abandoned buildings that can be seen now are what came in the next generation.

We went looking for Wostok initially because it was said to boast a picturesque Orthodox church. We found the church—like most of its kind, it was perched on the highest bit of land and did indeed offer a great vista over the fields, but was much smaller than I had anticipated.

Wostok itself had clearly never been a boomtown, even though the railroad once ran alongside it. We found no evidence of anything that might have been a train station, and not a lot of commerce. The few remaining buildings were small, framed with narrow boards—the shell of a general store was distinguished from the shell of an adjacent residence only by the windows on the front. A community hall, made of concrete and therefore presumably more recent, looked like it still saw occasional use. A couple of former farmhouses showed signs of habitation, in the form of vehicles and kids' toys outside.

The land, however, was still in agricultural use. We visited on a beautiful, early-summer day in 2020 when the grass was at the peak of greenness. It had rained heavily a few days before, but there were very few tire tracks in the soupy dirt roads, and no footprints by the fields where we stopped to look at the horses and cows. We could see the remains of sheds in the fields and assumed they were now being used to store animal feed.

During the twentieth century, when many of the homes and the farms were left to decay, dissolving into the greens and browns of the central Alberta countryside, the churches held on. In this part of the province, the old churches were mostly Eastern Catholic and Orthodox. Neither of those traditions is mine. I grew up as a nominal Christian in religious settings characterized by normative white Protestantism. In those spaces, Roman Catholicism functioned as the spiritual other: Christian enough to be familiar, but adorned with trappings and rituals that put it just beyond the pale of what was comfortable to WASPS. Catholicism seemed vaguely atavistic, a throwback to a time before the brisk, antiseptic straightforwardness of Methodism and Presbyterianism.

Moving to Alberta reminded me that othering is a matter of context. If I had grown up in Edmonton, the other to Canada's normative Protestantism would have been the Eastern Rite churches, whose theologies and aesthetics came to this part of the country in the late nineteenth through the mid-twentieth centuries, brought by immigrants from the non-Catholic and non-Protestant regions of Ukraine and Russia and Poland, as well as from countries that no longer exist.

In the racial and ethnic hierarchy of early settler Alberta, the Anglo Protestant elites considered the Slavs and eastern Europeans as only nominally white—a few cuts below the Catholic Germans and Portuguese, and maybe a step or two above people from India or China. The value of Slavic and eastern European immigrants, according to the political leaders of the province, lay in their physiological and agricultural fertility, or the myths thereof. The Slav peasants could be counted on to have dozens of sons and daughters, and they would till the scrubby land that Scottish and English immigrants and farmers from Ontario didn't want, turning it into wheat fields like the steppes of Russia. They would fill up the Canadian west with farms and descendants, pushing the Indigenous people out and forming a bulwark against incursions by land-hungry Americans from Montana or the Dakotas.

The settler elite of Alberta got the stalwart peasants they wanted, but they also got foreign churches and cathedrals and monasteries, filled with priests and monks with allegiances to clergy bearing strange titles like metropolitans or patriarchs. Immigrant families might have lived in sod dugouts, but they pooled their resources and built onion-domed churches wherever they could, and created or imported painted icons and gilded processional crosses. The power of the Orthodox Church in holding back the full assimilation of European immigrants into subjects of the British Empire was a topic of much concern to the new provincial civil service, and led to questions about the loyalties of the immigrants, especially during the First World War (notwithstanding that many of those who immigrated did so because life under the Russian czar or his allies was intolerable).

Time passes and social orders change, and today in Alberta the descendants of eastern European settlers wield considerable power.

The ranks of municipal and provincial politicians, generally on the conservative side of the spectrum, are filled with names like Zwozdesky and Hawrelak and Lukaszuk, and Edmonton is rife with speciality grocers selling perogies and cabbage rolls. Heritage groups and political lobbyists emphasize the cultural ties between Alberta and Poland or Ukraine. In the 2016 census, 17 per cent of Albertans identified their ethnic origins as Ukrainian, Polish, or Russian, although only 1.5 per cent claimed Ukrainian, Polish, or Russian as a mother tongue.

Living in Alberta, I got used to seeing Orthodox churches and basilicas in every town and city, and adjusted my expectation of religious holidays to include Orthodox Christmas and Orthodox Easter on different dates than the more familiar ones. I encountered some odd theological terms (what, exactly, is a *dormition*?) but overall, Orthodoxy blended into the scenery, as a counterpoint to the tidy white United Church buildings that I knew so well.

I gradually came to realize, however, that even Orthodoxy had its own other, and that was Eastern Catholicism. While the archetypal Ukrainian or Russian immigrant was Orthodox, a substantial minority attended Catholic churches. These looked nothing like the Catholic churches I was used to from eastern Canada. They were curvaceous, domed, rounded buildings, from the outside indistinguishable from their Orthodox counterparts. Eastern Rite Catholic churches even displayed the cross with three bars, unlike the single-barred Latin crosses of Western Catholic and Protestant churches. Often, the only way to tell that an eastern European immigrant community was divided between Catholic and Orthodox worshippers was by the presence of two churches built very close to each other. This brings me to Spaca Moskalyk.

Spaca Moskalyk is a three-domed, bell-towered, clapboard-walled, disused Ukrainian Catholic church in rural Lamont County, near Wostok. It sits in the midst of fields quadrisected by country roads, surrounded by a cemetery, two kilometres from its Orthodox twin, the Church of the Dormition of St. Mary. The land was donated by the Moskalyk farming family in 1924, the church went up in 1925, and a separate bell tower was added in 1938 as the congregation boomed. By the 1990s, the community of Ukrainian farmers was well into its third generation, but attendance at Sunday services had dwindled and the church was shuttered. In 2013, the county determined that the building had a disintegrating foundation and was unsafe. Officials recommended that the church be destroyed by fire, in the form of a controlled burn to reduce it to ashes. But former parishioners rallied. They raised money and hired a construction company to lift the entire building, move it a few metres, and set it down on top of a new foundation in 2016.

Perhaps because of the saved-from-the-flames story, Spaca Moskalyk has become modestly famous. It appears on internet listicles of amazing abandoned churches, alongside medieval cloisters in England and eight-hundred-year-old monasteries half-destroyed by earthquakes in Armenia. It also has a flourishing half-life in amateur online photography, accessible to anyone with the click of a mouse.

I spent hours looking at pictures of the church online, pictures that were usually shot dramatically from the ground upwards. I came to know its features: the white paint stippled with grey peels, the windows covered with boards, the clover-ended tarnished metal crosses above the doors, and the emptiness surrounding it. Big prairie skies provided the backdrop; the church was often silhouetted against a sunset or an incoming thunderstorm. It was the apotheosis of abandonment, a narrative of inhabitation and absence condensed into iconic images.

Spaca Moskalyk is not like some of the other disused or rarely used Orthodox churches that speckle the landscape. Lamont County is the Ukrainian immigrant heartland, once home to great influxes of church-going families. In other parts of the province, Ukrainian Catholic or Orthodox churches tend to be smaller and more visibly disused, like St. George's near Carvel or St. Michael's near Westlock, tucked into wooded corners rather than anchoring quarter-sections of active farmland. In the heartland, the churches were bigger and the congregations hung on to viability for longer.

When I actually got to visit Spaca Moskalyk on a wintry November weekend in 2021, on another expedition with my partner, it was different from what I expected. Primed by elaborately composed photos on Instagram and Flickr, I thought I would find the pinnacle of Alberta ruins, oozing glamour and decrepitude, but the church was smaller than it looked onscreen. The 2016 concrete foundation meant that it no longer listed erratically to one side. It had been freshly painted, and it was white, white, white, matching the snow. A chained gate prevented vehicles from getting too close, but someone had built a person-sized gate that could be squeezed around. Someone had also plowed the snow recently, so that approaching the church did not require sinking up to my thighs in drifts.

This place was being cared for. It was empty that day, but clearly not forgotten. It belonged to somebody, somewhere—perhaps the descendants of those laid to rest in the adjacent cemetery, beneath grave markers with Byzantine curves and flourishes? Maybe its care-takers were farm families who had moved to the nearby town of Mundare and now went to services, if they attended church at all, in the flat, boxy, 1960s-era Sts. Peter and Paul Ukrainian Catholic church on the main street. Spaca Moskalyk was still magnificent against the vivid blue sky, and the new white paint enhanced the contrast of colours in a way that the old greying and chipping paint had not—at least judging by the pictures I'd seen.

Up close and in three dimensions, I could appreciate the complex angles of the architecture. I marvelled at the skill and time it must have taken to juxtapose the boards just so, using narrow poplar planks in place of the brick and white limestone of the Russian churches that the builders must have remembered. Indeed, the wooden boards of Spaca Moskalyk reminded me of pictures of eighteenth-century churches in Siberia and other outposts of the Russian Empire, churches made of wood because other materials were too expensive or too far away.

Spaca Moskalyk sat in the space between abandoned and not-abandoned. The ghosts of care hovered around it. I had expected some-thing more ruined, but this building was not entirely deserted, just unused. Someone, or several someones, did not want it to decay completely, probably the same people who did not want it incinerated.

Its neighbours, abandoned farmhouses, were both ruined and deserted. We stopped at three such houses on the way back to the city, and clambered through soft muffles of snow to have a look at their interiors. Unlike the church, the farmhouses had doors that gave way with the slightest push of a hand, opening to reveal remnants of wallpaper, bedsprings, and stairways leading to narrow and cramped upper storeys. Two of the houses had been used for storage—the former parlours contained a few hay bales spilling straws; the old kitchens were filled with the wire frames of chicken coops. Rusted tin cans were clamped to the frames, which must have functioned as feeders.

These houses did not show up on any maps of the area, and there had been no attempts to fortify them against intruders. I could have stepped inside and wandered through the rooms, but I would have risked a plunge through rotten floorboards to whatever remained of the cellars. By this time of day, the late-afternoon light slanted through the windows, laying out golden oblongs on floors littered with hay and debris. The bits of straw shone. The pinkish curls of wallpaper took on a deeper, amber tone. It was beautiful, in its own way.

The people who used to care for these places were long gone. No one was keeping them up, or keeping them clean. No one was preserving them as expressions of a community, in the expectation of a revival when the doors might be opened again. It no longer mattered to anyone whether I went into these houses or remained safely on the perimeter, pacing around the overgrown thorn bushes.

Driving northwest from Spaca Moskalyk towards the Vinca Bridge was a short journey from the remains of the nineteenth century to the debris of the twenty-first. The Orthodox influence was still visible in the domes of tiny and dilapidated roadside churches, and the names of local secondary roads sounded Polish or Russian, but the dominant spirits in the area were those that propel enormous tanker trucks towards chemical plants, across terrain that looked only intermittently like farmland. This was a big-agriculture, industrial-chemical landscape, featuring gigantic metal cylinders for seed and fertilizer, and complicated railcar switching yards.

The whole district is known officially as the High Load Corridor, which refers to stretches of provincially maintained roads travelled by trucks that are both heavily loaded and vertically top-heavy—in other words, trucks carrying equipment to and from the oil and gas fields in the northeast, including the area around Fort McMurray. (I once travelled from Edmonton to Fort McMurray by road. Both coming and going, our nine-person van was constantly passed by labouring behemoths of tractor-trailers, carrying only slightly smaller vehicles and drilling rigs. Each truck looked like an insect with another insect on its back.)

High and heavy loads are hard on roads, especially in combination with temperature swings of 80 degrees between summer and winter. The surfaces of Lamont County roads are pocked with dips and craters, bruised by years of big trucks. The municipality of Sturgeon County, where the Vinca Bridge is located, had successfully petitioned the province to replace the old bridge with something that could bear the weight of these vehicles. The last time I had driven out to the area, however, in the summer of 2021, the project was already two years behind schedule.

That day, I pulled off into a shallow drive just on the Edmonton side of the river. I found an abandoned farmstead under the bridge itself, which hadn't been abandoned for long enough to slide into a complex relationship with the earth. The farmhouse was tagged with graffiti, missing its doors and windows, and the electrical wires had been recently stripped out. Next to it was a barn, with the remains of stalls. When I ventured in, I met a spate of flapping wings as pigeons took off and sensed a foot-level scurry that was probably a feral cat, its heft being too large for a mouse or a gopher. Nothing really to see here. The only thing that made the walk down to the water worthwhile was the North Saskatchewan River itself, broad and mirror-flat and tinted the turquoise colour of water that begins in the mountains.

Home for the Time Being

ONE OF THE VERY FEW GOOD THINGS about the COVID-19 pandemic is that it brought me back into communion with people I knew long ago. In the first few months, there was a brief flurry of reunions and reconnections, borne on currents of ambient anxiety and boredom, made possible by the new technologies those of us now working from home were mastering. It was fun for a while, but the novelty gradually wore off. Zoom didn't age well, and after months of conducting work entirely through the screen, the thought of more Zooming for the purpose of socializing had little appeal. There was one exception, however.

The exception was a group of eight people that I'd gone to junior high and high school with, all women, with whom I fell back into regular contact on Zoom and Messenger. The nine of us had met when we were just barely into puberty and now we were, good lord how does this happen, secured in the menopause. We weren't all part of the same inner circle, but we knew the details of one another's lives and we were friends. None of us were the popular girls, although some of us had pretty active social lives. We shared a common nerdiness back in the 1980s when being nerdy was not so cool, and as of 2020 we all craved connection and conversation with people who were not our fellow quarantine inmates.

I don't remember whose idea it was to start a group chat and then to message one another all the time, but it happened. We shared GIFS of shiba inus and videos of llamas, and some of the heavy stuff, too: several parental deaths as well as marital and adult-child-raising conundrums and career crises, all ratcheted up several degrees of intensity by COVID. It was, and still is, great. I am plugged back into a cohort, a network of people who have grown into the adults that were present in seedlike form forty-five years ago, a bit battered and world-weary but also efflorescent and smart.

I also don't remember who first suggested that we should combine our resources and create some sort of semi-off-grid commune, rural or urban, for our old age and the impending end of the world, like a cross between *Grizzly Adams* and *The Golden Girls*. We laughed about it, but we were all well educated and tuned in. We knew what was coming in the way of ecological apocalypse. Some of us were scientists who were immersed in the dire news of climate change on every working day.

The idea of the commune was a joke that hovered at the edge of being a plan. But the more we talked about it, the more sense it made. We were all outdoorsy in different ways, from teenage summers spent tree-planting to a career that involves scaling cliffs, and we had all independently converged on a sort of survivalist-lite approach to getting through the pandemic—an approach that extended to other emergencies and crises. We had created stockpiles of non-perishable food and had amassed a few more medical supplies than our households really needed. We had accumulated old copies of *The Foxfire Book* and *Where There Is No Doctor* over the years. Collectively, we had some useful skills—bread-making, gardening, putting solar arrays on roofs—and figured we could pick up others, as long as we could connect to the internet every now and then, before it went dark forever. In more pragmatic terms, we each had some financial resources that would go much further if we pooled them. That money could help us create a pleasant place to live, perhaps with thirty-six-inch doorways to accommodate mobility devices and a walk-out patio for our daily dose of sunshine and vitamin D. Partners and kids would be welcome in our survive-the-apocalypse commune, but the core group of residents would be the nine of us.

This sort of mutual aid, however whimsical or fantastical, seemed preferable to the eldercare arrangements we had witnessed or been part of. Our parents were in their eighties and nineties, and we had all been involved in patching together caregiving services or helping parents downsize into assisted-living facilities. Some parents made the transition happily, glad to be rid of the physical challenges and worries of keeping a single-family house going, but others withdrew into themselves or became fearful and resentful of the strangers among whom they would now live out the rest of their days.

By contrast, the prospect of seeing *out* our adult lives in the company of the people with whom we had seen them *in* had a symmetrical appeal. Many of us had already lost our parents, or were dealing with the crises of aging, and so the ends of things were more on our minds than they would have been a few decades ago. One friend noted that, in most forms of dementia, the last memories to go are the oldest ones. So with her parents deceased and no older siblings alive, we, her friends from grade seven, would probably be the last people she would recognize.

Where to put this fantasy commune? One possibility was to buy a derelict motel in Elliot Lake, Ontario—beautiful scenery! cross-country skiing right outside!—and fix it up. Unfortunately, we had all read *The Shining*, so that didn't get traction. I suggested we consider buying an eightplex, or a strip mall with apartments above it, along 101 Avenue in Edmonton. My theory was that 101 Avenue, in the few blocks to either side of 75 Street, was poised to become the Next Hot Neighbourhood, and we could finance any renovations with the rent we'd get from the gastropubs and artisanal soap stores that I was certain were going to start popping up like daffodils in the spring rain, in the storefront spaces beneath our residences. We could also open a life coaching and advice bureau for post-millennials in the area, mobilizing our considerable crone wisdom.

Then again, "life coaching and advice" describes much of the work we've been doing—for free—for our partners and kids over the past few decades, so it is deeply unappealing as a paying gig. I also have no track record as a real estate prognosticator, and it would be unwise for anyone to bank on my ability to spot the Next Hot Neighbourhood.

And, unfortunately, our neighbourhoods are getting hot in more ways than one. Underlying the entertainment value of imagining how we would all live in our crone commune, our discussions of the herbs we would learn to grow and the spruce beer we would brew, was the knowledge that all neighbourhoods were getting really hot, and might soon tip over from being merely uncomfortable in summer to being potentially lethal.

The futures we played with all had northernness stitched into them. Edmonton's searing minus-40 winters might sear a lot less before we came to the end of our lifespans. The farther north and west you go, the closer you are to glacial sources of fresh drinking water, which would be worth more than the remaining oil under the ground not far away. Even Elliot Lake's remoteness in Ontario might protect it from the permanent blanket of smog descending on the Golden Horseshoe, where a quarter of Canada's population lives.

Under all the banter and daydreams of renovated motels or survivalist-lite rural compounds, what we were talking about was having a home in the world, a home for the time being. The people make the home, so the saying goes, and we are all rich in partners, children, and friends. But a home is also a place, and the range of places that could serve as settings for our sunset years is getting smaller with each year that passes.

Packingtown

IN 2010 MY MARRIAGE had just come to an end, and I was looking for a new home to go with the new life I was embarking on, albeit not entirely of my own choice. I couldn't afford anything like the place we referred to in legalese as the "matrimonial home": a detached single-family residence on a decently sized lot in one of central Edmonton's more desirable neighbourhoods. My purchasing options were clear. I could buy an older house in a central neighbourhood (one that needed the kind of dedicated time and money that I didn't have in order for it to be halfway comfortable); I could buy a new-ish house in the suburbs, on a winding road or cul-de-sac far from the central Edmonton numbered street grid; or I could buy a unit in a multi-family development somewhere, whether townhouse or apartment.

Fortunately for me, having nowhere to live was not one of the options; neither was moving into an unsafe or unstable living situation, so I was luckier than many women who leave marriages in midlife. I started calling realtors, checking with friends who'd moved recently, and scanning the city with a new eye, one attuned to the possibility that the next few decades might be very different from the last few. A change would do me good.

It was in this spirit of *incipit vita nova* that I began gathering information about a proposed new development in northeast Edmonton, which I'll call Green Point. This development was supposed to be literally groundbreaking, a new enterprise in a thinly populated part of

< *Smokestack from the Canada Packers plant, built in 1936, in Edmonton, Alberta.* (Photo by the author.)

Edmonton that had gone into the sort of decline I associate with the Rust Belt cities of Michigan and Ohio, deindustrialization and disinhabitation. It was to be located along Fort Road, a traffic artery that slices diagonally through the right-angled grid of city streets, parallel with the railroad tracks.

I knew the area mainly from working at charity bingos at the Fort Road Bingo Hall and from hauling carloads of recyclables to the bottle depots dotting the empty asphalt lakebeds where businesses connected to the railroad once stood. The only landmark I knew was the hundred-year-old Transit Hotel, one of the scattering of old residential hotels in formerly industrial parts of Edmonton that clung to economic viability by offering 24/7 happy hours and cheap vodka in the off-sales outlet. All I knew about the Transit Hotel, as distinct from its siblings like the Commercial or the Dover, was that it was supposed to have a haunted barbershop in the basement, and that people used to bet on gerbil races in the bar.

The Green Point community, judging by the promotional information and brochures I received, would transform the area. It would have townhouses, apartment buildings, and residential-above-retail precincts, with rooftop gardens, playgrounds, and outdoor gathering spaces. It would be walkable and transit-oriented, with easy access to the big northeast LRT stations, Belvedere and Clareview, which feed into downtown Edmonton. Artists' renderings of a typical day in Green Point showed a festival of people—parents with children, elders, youth, pairs and trios and quartets of friends—under a sunny sky, congregating in the village green or heading off for the train. It wasn't hard to figure out why these scenes of conviviality resonated with me at that moment, in the throes of my relationship disintegration.

Green Point also had me at "green." Back when I was trading emails with the project's developers, I still hadn't seen the word *emergency* attached to *climate*, and I thought of environmental responsibility in terms of keeping the soil and water clean rather than in terms of a planet inexorably boiling. Nevertheless, I knew that overconsumption by wealthy Canadians was a big problem, and I was therefore drawn to new ideas or possibilities that might hold some of the solution. Green

Point was promoted as being one of Canada's first entirely passively heated residential developments. Passive heating, achieved through the use of solar panels (to generate electricity), solar thermal technology (to heat water), and greater efficiency (better insulation, plus those eye-catching green roofs) would reduce energy consumption by up to 90 per cent. There was also something called an "invisible building" water cycle, which I didn't quite grasp, except that it involved harvesting rainwater as well as recycling and reusing as much household water as possible.

In addition to the eco-halo, I can't deny that the location of the development was part of its draw. I fell prey to the quintessentially settler-western desire to set out for the frontier, to bring sociality to a remote and beleaguered place, only now with a tint of gentrification. I was thoroughly interpellated by the promotional material for Green Point, which struck a high-minded pioneer chord:

> You'll be the first of 112 to set down roots in the same spot many did over 100 years ago. As you settle into your new home, you'll be joined by many retailers looking to take part in the urban renewal. You'll be joined by many new neighbors as we build more buildings around [Green Point], we plan to bring life, families, seniors and friends together...it's the story of the future that we need your help writing, be a part of the urban transformation and know you're part of something very special.

I loved imagining that my daughter and I would go boldly off to the northeast, a part of the city that, at the time, was regarded as much less than desirable by the people I hung around with. Now, well over a decade later, I can see what I didn't see then, how my desires to reclaim and rebuild were not so far off the colonizing impulse that had deformed the history of this place, how the idea of myself as an urban pioneer on the post-industrial green frontier was more than a little bit self-mythologizing.

In any event, the move to Green Point never happened. I waited for months to receive prospectuses with dollar figures attached, and then agonized over whether to commit a down payment to something that had yet to manifest itself in a shovel in the dirt. I ended up buying an apartment-style condo in the southeast-central part of the city instead.

Over the next few years, I kept an eye on that section of Fort Road, watching for hints of what might have been. There wasn't a lot to see. The Fort Road Redevelopment Association signs gradually faded; their corners came untacked and flapped in the winter squalls. A couple of the major thoroughfares were repaved. The Burger Baron and the all-you-can-eat buffet closed and stood vacant, while the Transit Hotel reopened as a barbecue joint with a slightly expanded beer menu.

In the meantime, the Green Point development fell further and further behind schedule, and the partnership between the City of Edmonton and the private companies that were to build the homes got more and more tangled. Complaining letters started to turn up in the *Edmonton Journal*, lamenting that the·grand plans (and the expropriation of businesses on routes intended to be used for Green Point) had come to nothing.

Underlying the delays was the problem of the area's brownfields, its literal physical underlayer. Brownfields are contaminated lands that carry the toxic residue of former commercial and industrial activities, residue that has rendered them at least temporarily unusable. Spills, leaks, waste dumping, slow leaching and accidental breaching of containments put pollutants into the dirt and water, and these contaminants remain even after the industry or the business has moved on or died off, even after no one remembers what used to be there. Dry cleaners, photo finishers, metalwork shops, storage facilities, and feedlots all leave their marks.

The neighbourhood where I live now is dotted with very small brownfields, almost all of which are the ghosts of former gas stations. When I first moved in, the remains of an old gas station that hadn't operated in decades could still be seen a few blocks away. The building had a brief re-awakening as a party supply store that sold balloons and tanks of helium, but it was later left to collapse. The land was reclaimed a few years later to house a craft brewery and a small-batch coffee roaster.

Just a block from where I live was a fast-food place that had become something of a local legend and then decayed into a brownfield. In the early 2000s, Charles Smart Donair, as it was called, went through enormous quantities of ground lamb and beef every weekend. It even appeared in roadside-attractions guides for having the world's largest meat cone, a five-hundred-pound pile on a roasting spit, six feet tall.

Charles Smart closed around the time I moved into the neighbourhood. Its open kitchen and eating area with moulded plastic seats sat undisturbed for a few years before the whole thing was razed and became a vacant lot, which it remains today. The demise of the business was attributed to culinary infighting among the founders' sons, but the abandonment of the place, which should have been prime real estate, was due to the soil being contaminated with cooking grease and the residue of all the sheep and cattle who were turned into donairs in the two decades of its existence. This is what I've heard from older neighbours. I don't know if it's true.

The fate of Charles Smart was not very different from the fate of the northeast Edmonton industrial brownfields, across the North Saskatchewan River, where the urban eco-village of Green Point was supposed to rise triumphant from contaminated land. The Fort Road area used to be called Packingtown, as it was once the centre of Edmonton's slaughterhouse and meatpacking industry. Meatpacking began in this location with the Swift packinghouse in 1908, and the shacks and small houses that accommodated the mainly immigrant workforce were briefly incorporated as the Village of North Edmonton, before it became nominally part of Edmonton itself in 1912. The Transit Hotel opened in 1908, boasting the only running water in the neighbourhood, and the first churches arrived in 1909, holding services for their congregations in the upper storey of the general store before their own buildings were completed.

All those cowboy dreams of rural Alberta, all those great ranches of the prairies and the badlands, needed somewhere to send their cattle to be killed and packaged, and for the first half of the twentieth century, Packingtown was that somewhere. According to Alberta labour historian

Kevin Bell, Packingtown was the second largest meatpacking site in North America, following Chicago's notorious Union Stock Yards. Meatpacking was the dirty, smelly, noisy, and unromantic side of an agricultural economy, and it's no coincidence that Packingtown was located on what was then the outermost edge of Edmonton, close to the Canadian Northern Railway and Grand Trunk Railway lines but far away (and downwind) from the main residential parts of the city.

I'd never given much thought to the cultural meanings of meatpacking before I started to poke around my would-be new neighbourhood, when I began dreaming of the fresh start I could make at Green Point. I learned that, as urban activities go, meatpacking is liminal in every way.

In geographic terms, meatpacking districts were typically on the perimeters of residential neighbourhoods; all they shared with the more affluent urban districts was their dependence on the railroads. Once large-scale commercial trucking and refrigeration effectively cut that dependence, slaughterhouses and meatpacking plants moved to smaller, out-of-the-way rural areas like Oelwein, Iowa, or Garden City, Kansas. In Alberta, the biggest slaughtering and packing plants are now in the southern part of the province, at High River and Brooks.

Meatpacking districts in larger cities became anachronisms, and the killing floors and warehouses either fell into decline or were repurposed. In New York City, "the meatpacking district" was shorthand for the area and its activities that should not, or could not, go on under the eyes of the respectable bourgeois. In the mid-twentieth century, the district morphed into a sanctuary for sexual minorities, mainly gay men, after the meatpackers moved out of west Manhattan, where railroads had been bringing in cattle since the 1860s.

Commercial meatpacking is also a historically liminal activity, one that emerged at the early edges of the Industrial Revolution in Europe. Butchery, making one's livelihood through the craft of cutting up meat, had been around even before the surges of population into the cities, but in agrarian communities, most animals that were to be slaughtered for meat were either killed in the households where they were consumed, or sold to local butchers who killed, dressed, and sold the meat in the same community.

Public abattoirs had existed since the Middle Ages (an Old English name for the village butcher's market is the *shambles*), but the big commercial meatpacking corporation, with its concomitant division of slaughterhouse work into specialized tasks, was the product of population concentration in urban areas as well as the rise of wage labour, which generated a demand for meat among people who did not raise their own animals. In the late nineteenth and early twentieth centuries, the industrial philosophy of Taylorism—which required breaking down labour processes into repetitive tasks to maximize efficiency and minimize diversity—took hold in the "disassembly lines" of the meatpacking plants, even before it spread to manufacturing and the assembly lines of car and appliance manufacturers.

So, meatpacking—smelly, cold, socially marginal, and, thanks to the disassembly line, deskilled, compared with the older trade of the butcher. But also, in Edmonton as in other western cities, it was one of the last bastions of the good working-class job: unionized, well paid, and secure, especially for new arrivals. In 2015, the Edmonton arts organization Ground Zero Productions began to collect oral histories from people who had worked in the city's meatpacking plants in their heyday. These men and women described the heavy work of hauling carcasses in cold, wet work areas, the bits of fingers they lost to saws, and the constant hurry-up of the disassembly line. But they also talked about decades of reliable employment, unions that protected their jobs, and community life centred on the personal connections developed in the plants. They talked about working in the cafés that served meals to shift workers in the 1940s and 1950s, riding bikes on the dirt roads that linked the residential areas, and using frozen horse manure for hockey pucks in the impromptu ice rinks that sprang up around the Transit Hotel. In their voices, there's melancholy: a nostalgia for a community that disappeared.

Edmonton's meatpacking industry started to decline in the 1980s, largely because of competition from abattoirs and meat plants in smaller population centres with fewer unions and lower wages. The death blow was dealt by Peter Pocklington, an Edmonton magnate and moneybags villain out of a left-wing comic strip, who bought the

Gainers meatpacking business in 1979, and by 1986 had forced the union into a six-month-long job action over wages. (Pocklington also owned the Edmonton Oilers hockey team, where he paid million-dollar salaries. Oilers players could make more in an evening—without even winning—than a Gainers line worker could make in a year.)

In 1986 I was a student in Montreal, but I remember the Gainers strike dominating national headlines and TV news broadcasts, with aggressive on-camera showdowns between the strike-breakers and the striking workers. One of my left-wing student buddies had a pro-labour sticker on their fridge, and the slogan was repulsive enough that I remember it forty years later: Gainers Makes Wieners With Scabs.

The strike ended when workers ran out of time and money, and the prospect of a cold winter on the picket lines loomed. They accepted a contract brokered by the provincial government that gave them no wage gains. Within ten years, Pocklington had shut down the Gainers plant entirely, and handed the defunct facility over to the province after defaulting on a government loan to keep the doors open. The plant was demolished and its abandoned lands, contaminated with literal blood, sweat, and tears, were eventually taken over by the city.

Today, Packingtown has been all but obliterated, in a display of geographic amnesia that's extraordinary even by Edmonton standards. Back when I was looking at Green Point's futuristic renderings, I also looked at the provincial archives' collection of pictures from the former Village of North Edmonton, when Fort Road was a commercial thoroughfare and the packing plants were humming. With these images in mind, I set out to explore the neighbourhood. At that time, I saw almost no trace of either the industrial past or the imagined green future. The residential buildings were mainly 1950s low-rise apartments and split-level fourplexes. The commercial properties were low-slung oblongs fronted by big parking lots and pockmarked with vacancies.

The only recognizable landmarks were the Transit Hotel and the single remaining smokestack from the Canada Packers plant, a brick finger to the sky surrounded by open fields littered with dumped rubble. In the ambitious redevelopment plans for the area, several of which have come and gone in the last two decades, the smokestack is meant to serve as a sort of icon or totem for the area, a memory of its industrial past. But nothing much has been done with it. A historic plaque states that it is, indeed, a smokestack, which is evident to anyone looking at it, and provides some architectural and engineering information about the building it used to be attached to.

Then I went back in 2022, and saw more. The area is changing. It hasn't undergone the transformation envisaged in the Green Point plans I pored over, dreaming of rooftop gardens and solar heat, but it's not just the brownfield vacuum of the former Packingtown. The biggest new building is the Kathleen Andrews Transit Garage, named for the city's first female bus driver. It's a surprisingly pretty building, in a style that I think of as northern winter naturalism, with waves of steel that shimmer and reflect the grey November sky, and wire cubes several times the height of a person, packed with jagged grey and white rocks. Signs of life have also appeared in the strip malls and service roads off Fort: the Honey Bunny Christian Daycare has moved into a light industrial area, and in among the bottle depots and pawnshops, I saw the shoots of an African shopping district, with grocery and beauty supply stores.

I also saw the version of Green Point that became a reality, a version that has little to do with the original brochures and mailouts. Compared with the promise, it's tiny. It's a block-long building with four floors of apartments over street-level shops, green and yellow and red. It's all rental—the developers tried to pitch it as a condo project but didn't find enough buyers. The rest of the Green Point land remains empty; signs encourage prospective investors to get in touch with the city. The local paper still runs sporadic editorials and letters from frustrated residents and business owners in adjoining neighbourhoods who are tired of seeing the lonely smokestack surrounded by weeds and puddles. The land waits in the twilight, without the industry workers that once filled it up or the urban villagers who were intended to replace them.

And as for me, just like almost everyone else who once had a history or a dream of the future in these now-empty fields, I've moved on.

The Most Important Things Have Already Happened

I'M A SOCIOLOGY PROFESSOR, and when I teach the sociology of families, I talk about the idea of a normative life course. That's the notion that there are certain events one can expect to experience, certain relationships and transformative moments, and that these proceed chronologically in a more or less straightforward fashion— love, marriage, baby carriage, and so forth. What exactly these events are, and how and when they unfold, is not fixed by natural law but variable, according to the cultural prescriptions that infiltrate our imaginations.

Literature and movies and all manner of popular culture are built around these events. The life course is the scaffolding that holds up the plot of the rom-com, the bildungsroman, the Hallmark holiday special. In movies and books and on TV, the protagonist is always *about to* have these things happen to them. The first love, the marriage, the baby, the life-changing moment, whatever it is, invariably lies in their near future, so we readers and viewers can experience it along with them, vicariously. By contrast, there aren't many movies or stories about older people who have already been through all of that. We don't lend ourselves as easily to certain plot devices as the young do, for whom most of the significant material of life lies still ahead and is therefore mysterious and fascinating. (This is not to say older adults don't exist in movies and books—we do—but the marriage plot, the love plot, the coming-of-age plot are not the plots in which we're front and centre.) The characters from our cohort, to whom these things have either already happened or will never happen, are just slightly tangential to the younger characters whose lives are still full of narrative potential.

It's odd to be of an age when most of the important things that happen to people, according to the culturally emplotted normative life course, have already happened to me. I've been the child in a parent-child relationship and received all the parental attention and interest that I will ever receive. I've been married (once) and had a child (once), and neither of those things will happen again (definitely not the child; the marriage is not impossible). I know who my first love was and who my best friend is. I've fallen in love a couple of times and probably won't fall in love again. I know what my career is, was, will be. I'm pretty sure I know where I'm going to live for the rest of my life, which is here in Alberta. I unwrap these certainties and turn them over, feel their weight and think, *All right, that's what that is. This is how my life has turned out.*

This knowing, this awareness that most of the important things in my life have already happened, doesn't mean I despair of the possibility of change. I am not the person I was five or ten years ago, and certainly not the person I will be five or ten years from now. I haven't extinguished the possibility of discovery, of transformation, and I'm optimistic, even as the years remaining to me tick down.

Those changes that lie ahead will be acts of re-invention, not of invention, not the inception of new lives. As I get older, I haven't withdrawn from curiosity, nor have I lost the capacity to see things anew. But seeing something anew is not the same as seeing it for the first time. I don't have a lot of blank spaces remaining in the book of my life, so the writing I do these days is really overwriting or re-writing.

I'm reminded of the nineteenth-century European epistles I saw in a museum, from a time when paper was precious. If you were writing a letter, you had only a finite number of pages to use. If the things you needed to say exceeded the paper available, you would turn your page ninety degrees and write crossways over your earlier works, or you'd turn it upside down and write in the spaces between the lines. Everything you wrote, once you'd filled the page for the first time, would be read over what had gone before it, your earlier words seeping through the later ones.

In the same way, my experiences in my forties and fifties—making friends, keeping friends, losing friends, impossible crushes, moments of sublimity in the wilderness, intellectual sparks catching fire, small comforts, and large detours—are overwritten on memories of earlier times. Later life is inscribed over earlier life, so that nothing is written for the first time, on the blank page. Words are infinite, but pages are numbered. I'm making the best use I can of my pages, writing the stories over and over, in the margins and crosswise, so that I can no longer discern the first story, the original words.

Holy Transfiguration

CEMETERIES ARE TIME TRAVEL. They collapse past and present into gravestones and inscriptions. The people are gone, but the bare facts of their existence—birth, marriage, death—remain long after the fullness of that existence has evaporated. However, the facts of that existence are never simple. They're woven into historical contingencies—who belonged to what place, whose life began and ended under what conditions, whose names are grouped together in death, and why.

Rural Alberta is dotted with these small cities of the dead, often attached to churches once vibrant but now gone quiet as congregations have aged and moved on. My partner and I like to wander the range roads and township roads in search of churches and old graveyards. One Saturday in October 2022, we came across the Holy Transfiguration Russo-Greek Orthodox Church, near the hamlet of Star, in Lamont County.

In the church's well-tended, pine-shaded cemetery, gravestones record the lives of Ukrainian settlers and their descendants from the late nineteenth century to the early twenty-first. The oldest are inscribed in Ukrainian using Cyrillic script, the more recent are bilingual (Ukrainian and English) using Roman script, and the most recent are only in English. Some of the gravestones from the early twentieth century are embellished with black-and-white studio photos of the

< Gravestone in the cemetery of Holy Transfiguration Russo-Greek Orthodox Church, near Star, Alberta. (Photo by the author.)

deceased in their prime, whereas newer ones are engraved with trac-
tors, fishing rods, or bouquets of flowers.

When I'm visiting old graveyards, I read the names on the gravestones and I move along. Unless the deceased were connected to me
in some particular way, which almost all the deceased of Alberta are
not, they have no individual existence in my memory. Their names
flow through my consciousness, a stream of first names, family names,
and nicknames, and then they're gone. They register for only a
moment. I leave them behind when I leave the graveyard.

I found Michael Chernyk's grave right in the middle of the cemetery, next to his wife Anna's, under a tamarack tree. His stone shows
his name and birth and death dates in Cyrillic, and features a photograph of Michael as a serious middle-aged man, possibly in his fifties.
On the obverse of his gravestone, someone had inscribed:

> *Sister of Michael Chernyk*
> *Married at age 14*
> *Died in the Ukraine of child birth*
> *Mother to*
> *Demetro 1887–1889*
> *Anna 1889–1910*
> *Yawdoha 1891–1907 Pneumonia* TB
> *John 1894–1964*
> *Petro 1896– 2 years Scarlet fever*
> *Fred 1899–1986 Cancer*
> *Petro 1904– 3 month Pneumonia*

When we left the Holy Transfiguration Cemetery that day, what I took
along with me was the absence of a name, an un-name, or the negative
space where a name might have been. This absence is Michael Chernyk's
sister, who, if the anonymous engraver is right, never left Ukraine, gave
birth to seven children beginning in her teens, and saw two of them
die as toddlers. These austere bits of information were chiselled onto
her brother's gravestone sometime after 1986, when Fred, the longest-
lived of her children, died at the age of eighty-seven.

Who was Michael Chernyk's sister? I tried to find out. Thanks to online census records and genealogical databases—and the patient amateur historians who upload pieces of their stories—I was able to learn quite a lot about the people who came to rest in this cemetery, but not about her.

I learned that Michael (or Mihail) Chernyk (or Czernik) was born in November 1863, in the village of Nebyliv, in what was then Galicia, in a region called known as Prykarpattia. At different points, Prykarpattia has been part of Ukraine, Poland, the Kingdom of Galicia, the Austro-Hungarian Empire, the USSR (as part of the Ukrainian Soviet Socialist Republic), and, for eight months in 1918, it was part of the West Ukrainian People's Republic. These shifting boundaries are reflected in the way Chernyk's birthplace is recorded on genealogy websites: variously as Poland, Austria, Ukraine, Russia, and Galicia.

Fortunately for me, Nebyliv is one of the villages chosen by the Ukrainian Cultural Heritage Village, about half an hour east of Edmonton, as a model for its open-air museum of turn-of-the-century Ukrainian settler life, and so a few fragments of information have been preserved.

Michael Chernyk's early life is blank. I couldn't find any Chernyks or Czerniks in the family list that the Ukrainian Village maintains, but I did find a village called Chernyk about eighty kilometres from Nebyliv. I went to Ancestry.ca, searching for Chernyks from Nebyliv, hoping to find Michael. I found one person whose names and dates matched. On the associated family tree, the names of this Michael's parents are given as Joannes and Evdokia, but a search for those names turns up nothing (or, at least, nothing indexed in English). I found no information about brothers or sisters, including the sister whose story appears on his gravestone. And I could not trace either of Michael's two nephews who survived to adulthood, his sister's sons, who would presumably have carried the surname of their father, whoever he was.

Nebyliv today is so small as to be almost invisible on maps. But in Lamont County, one of the biggest nodes of Ukrainian immigration in Canada, Nebyliv is acknowledged as a wellspring of local history, marked by a recent twinning agreement between Nebyliv and the Town of Lamont. The official twinning ceremony took place in August 2021. By

March 2022, however, the Nebyliv region was under attack by invading Russian forces, and Lamont officials fretted publicly that they had lost contact with their counterparts in Ukraine. I tried to find out more about what the Russian invasion had meant for Nebyliv, but found nothing in the news.

But back to the nineteenth century. Michael Chernyk would have been twenty-eight in 1891, when Wasyl Eleniak and Ivan Pylypow, the first men to leave Nebyliv for what is now Alberta, sailed to Canada to investigate rumours of free farmland for white European settlers. According to genealogical databases, Michael would have been married for five years already to Anna Trynchy, also of Nebyliv, who had been only sixteen at the time of the wedding.

Michael would have been twenty-nine when Pylypow made the return trip to Nebyliv to tell neighbours that the rumours were true, there was land for the taking. Groups of men and married couples gradually filtered from Nebyliv and the surrounding areas into Canada. Once they arrived, many worked as hired hands for earlier Prykarpattia immigrants in Manitoba before moving west and taking land in Treaty 6 territory, the home of the Cree and Blackfoot.

Michael and Anna Chernyk stayed behind for more than a decade after the first settlers left Nebyliv for Canada West. According to a passenger manifest, the couple and their five children sailed from Hamburg aboard the ss *Armenia*, which arrived in Halifax on June 1, 1903. At that point, they enter the realm of Canadian censuses and it gets easier to pick up their traces. Their sixth child, Anna, was born in Lamont in 1904, the same year Michael's anonymous sister back in Galicia died. In 1909, Michael and Anna's seventh and final child, William, was also born in Lamont.

Unlike Michael's seven nephews and nieces, his own seven children were born at intervals of several years—the entire siblingship was drawn out over two decades, from 1890 to 1909. Also unlike his sister's children, Michael's children appear to have all lived well into their eighties. His two youngest daughters married men from anglophone settler families, judging by their husbands' surnames. His oldest daughter and all four of his sons appear to have married fellow Ukrainians (or Galicians, or Austrians, or Poles, or Russians) in Canada.

The Chernyk family appears as the Czerniks in the 1916 Canadian census. They were listed as farmers who lived a two-room log cabin in Lamont, adjacent to the families whose daughters the Czernik boys would marry. The 1916 census-taker notes that all members of the Czernik household could speak English, but according to the 1921 census-taker, Anna could not read or write. Michael died in 1941; Anna outlived him by fifteen years and was buried next to him in the Holy Transfiguration Cemetery. Three of their children are also buried there.

There is no indication as to when or why Michael's sister's details were added to his gravestone. This is the heart of the mystery: what led to Michael Chernyk's sister being remembered with an inscription on the marker for someone else's grave, thousands of kilometres from where she died, in a language she would not have been able to read? I had questions.

To begin with, why is the sister's name missing? Was her early marriage considered disgraceful or shameful? (Then again, Michael's wife was only two years older when she married him.) And if it was shameful or deviant, why put the sister's details out in public at all? Another possibility: sometimes names are deliberately lost. Sometimes, to refer to a person or a thing directly is considered dangerous, so a taboo occludes the actual name. The English word *bear* may derive from just such a taboo—it comes from an old Germanic word meaning "the brown one." Even further back in European history, the ancient Greek female spirits of wrath and retribution were called the Eumenides, or the kindly ones, rather than their true names, the Erinyes or Furies.

Could this be true for Michael Chernyk's sister? Was her name considered taboo? It seems unlikely. She was a child bride in an obscure town who didn't survive her fourth decade, not an avenging Fury.

Was her name simply forgotten? That, too, seems unlikely. If the person who carved the inscription knew that her last surviving child died in 1986, and that he died of cancer, surely this means there must have been some communication between the branches of the extended family over the decades. They weren't completely estranged.

I think it's more likely that her namelessness is deliberate, that it's part of the story the gravestone carver was trying to tell—that her individuality was less important than her fate.

If this is true, Michael Chernyk's sister is part of a long tradition of identifying women only by their marital and reproductive circumstances, whether benevolent or harrowing. Her namelessness fits into a gendered tradition of anonymity. I'm reminded of Virginia Woolf's speculation about the possibility of Shakespeare's sister, as well as the second-wave feminist T-shirt slogan "Anonymous Was a Woman."

More recently, Margaret Atwood's naming convention in *The Handmaid's Tale*, in which women of a particular class are known only as the property of the man who sires children by them, picks up this tradition and associates it explicitly with childbearing. Atwood's dystopia is intended as a cautionary tale, a time-honoured narrative genre. Is that the genre of this truncated, staccato account on Michael Chernyk's gravestone, of early marriage, rapid childbirths, and death after death?

Who is the imagined readership for this tale? The inscription appears in a western Canadian cemetery, in English, surrounded by the final resting places of people well-off enough to afford substantial carved headstones. Is it meant to be a story of progress? A way of comparing the backwardness of the old country with the modernity of the new? There were no such child marriages in Canada, at least not legal ones, and while I saw many grave makers in Holy Transfiguration for dead infants, a family losing four out of seven children before adulthood would be unusual in this community. Did the fate of Michael Chernyk's sister and her children represent the existence that the settlers thought they had left behind, one of anonymity and loss, followed by early death? Is the sister's fate an index of how far the Chernyks and their neighbours had travelled, in both geographical and cultural terms?

If so, it would harmonize with the larger narratives of the immigrant community that are preserved in writing, in artifacts, and in official recognition of Galician-Ukrainians moving from the old world into the new-to-them world (and in the process, displacing the Blackfoot and

Cree, who appear only briefly in censuses as "native" households). The very existence of the land I had been standing on, Holy Transfiguration itself, is part of that narrative.

The story of Holy Transfiguration really begins three hundred years before the first Ukrainian settlers arrived in Alberta, when the Kingdom of Poland pushed into what is now western Ukraine, bringing with it Greek Catholicism as the state religion. This led to the downgrading of Orthodoxy for generations. The new state religion was a rite of Catholicism that uses many of the same practices as Orthodox churches, but that, crucially for Polish and Austro-Hungarian rulers of this part of Ukraine, acknowledges the pope, rather than the Orthodox patriarch in Moscow or Kiev, as the head of the faith. The 1900 census data for Nebyliv shows 2,000 inhabitants, of whom 1,950 are listed as "Greek Catholic" (the rest were mainly Jewish, with a sprinkling of non-Greek Catholics). It's reasonable to assume that Michael Chernyk started out life as a Greek Catholic, at least nominally.

Some emigrants who left Galicia in the late nineteenth century carried their Catholicism with them, but others took the opportunity to revert to Orthodoxy, which they associated with the ancestral past and with the dream of an independent Ukraine to come. Ivan Pylypow, one of the two first Ukrainian-speaking settlers in Lamont, is described as having grown up in the Greek Catholic faith in Nebyliv, yet he and his wife and children are buried in the Orthodox cemetery. (His Nebyliv neighbour and fellow traveller Wasyl Eleniak, however, is buried with his wife and children in a Catholic cemetery in Lamont.) I think it's therefore likely that the Czerniks or Chernyks were originally Catholics, and possibly latecomers to Orthodoxy, post-emigration.

If the Nebyliv settlers started out as Catholics, the Catholicism that these settlers found in Canada would have seemed strange. Canadian priests were celibate, unlike their Prykarpattia counterparts who were expected to marry; they celebrated mass in Latin rather than Greek or Old Slavonic (the two church languages that Galicians would have encountered before emigrating); and they didn't know or understand the elements of the Byzantine way of doing things that had found their way into the state-sponsored Greek Catholicism of the old country.

In 1897, a group of Ukrainian settlers in Lamont petitioned the Orthodox bishop of Alaska and the Aleutian Islands, Nicholas Ziorov, to be received into the Orthodox Church on the strength of their ancestral Orthodoxy. Ziorov promptly dispatched two missionaries to Alberta to prepare the way for the nominally Catholic settlers to (re)join the Orthodox Church. These Orthodox missionaries jostled with missionary priests from the Catholic Church in Galicia, who were sent to follow the emigrants after word got back to Galicia that former Catholics were taking up Orthodoxy in their new country.

Shortly after the turn of the century, relations in Lamont between the settlers who had remained Catholic and those who had converted to Orthodoxy gradually broke down. The catalyst was the completion of the Holy Transfiguration church, which raised the question of which denomination would own the finished building and would conduct services in it according to their rite. The quarrel led to a Canadian court case over which group the building belonged to and therefore who was entitled to use it for Easter worship. Ultimately, the matter went to the Privy Council in England, who ruled in 1913 that the building was properly Orthodox; the Catholics moved down the road to a new church. Holy Transfiguration was reconfigured as a beacon of Orthodoxy, with icons, a bell-house, and travelling choirs, until it closed to regular services in the 1990s, as the rural Ukrainian-descended population declined.

This is the story as it's told by the Russian Orthodox sources I found—the backwardness of Galicia with its Catholicism enforced by Polish and Austro-Hungarian overlords, the trip to Canada and freedom, the embrace of Orthodoxy, which was also a return to Orthodoxy, made possible by emigration. But this is not the only story.

Reading a bit further, I learned that secular Ukrainian nationalists, active in the nineteenth century in the Ukrainian-speaking parts of Poland and Austria-Hungary, including Prykarpattia, viewed Orthodox churches with suspicion. They saw them as tentacles of the Russian Empire under the czar, and no more suitable to a free Ukraine than the enforcement of Greek Catholicism. The move that the Lamont settlers made to Orthodoxy might therefore be read not as an expression of spiritual self-determination but as a move from the frying pan to the fire, from one imperial faith to another.

In 2022, reading about the move from Catholicism to Orthodoxy by the early settlers was fraught with terrible historical irony. At the time, the armed forces of Russia were bombing and burning western Ukraine and had cut off water supplies to Kiev. They were doing this with the blessing of Patriarch Kirill, the head of the Russian Orthodox Church. The Church to which the Ukrainian-speaking settlers in Lamont turned when they arrived in Canada was urging the Russian army onwards in a war against the descendants of the people they left behind.

As I plowed through books and hyperlinked historical accounts of Ukrainian immigration to Canada and the intricacies of liturgical differences between Eastern Rite Catholicism and Eastern Rite Orthodoxy, layered over the political histories of Poland and the Austro-Hungarian and Russian empires, I realized that I had gone from trying to grasp the story of a person to trying to grasp the story of a place—from the mystery of Michael Chernyk's sister to the story of the cemetery itself and how it came to be holy land in this corner of Lamont County.

These stories came together in the inscription on Michael Chernyk's gravestone. The decision, by persons unknown, to inscribe the reproductive history of an anonymous Chernyk family member who died in Galicia, likely in the same year that her brother arrived in Alberta, must be connected somehow to a broader effort to write or rewrite the history of the community. But exactly how these stories are connected remains murky.

I still don't know who Michael Chernyk's sister was. The extraordinary and heartbreaking profligacy of seven lives begun and four ended in childhood was a piece in the great game of collective story-making. What mattered most to the person who inscribed her details—in a place she would never see, never know about—was not who she was, but that she and her children stayed in Ukraine and died; her brother and his children came to Canada and lived.

Standing Pose

GROWING OLD GRACEFULLY is supposed to involve calming and quieting the agitation of earlier years. The paragons of aging in popular culture are the serene and wise people—Buddhist sages, Obi-Wan Kenobi, definitely not King Lear. Yet as I move towards the far end of middle age, I'm constantly beset by restlessness of both psychic and physical forms.

When I am most beset, I feel like I'm made of a thousand tiny claws scrabbling to get a grip on something solid. This feeling is crossed with a constant subvocal hum warning me that there is something I should be doing or should have done that I am not doing or have not done (beyond the pointless scrabbling, of course). It's the drive to get something done right, to accomplish something good while I still can, paired with the knowledge that I'm living in the prologue to ill-health, incapacity, and eventually death. The claws and the hum are perhaps part of the temporality of being an aging person who is conscious that time is not infinite, or perhaps it's broader than that: it's the temporality of a mortal human who is aware that the future is becoming the past, and doing so very quickly.

I used to do a lot of yoga—I was not devoted to it, and I did not have a dedicated practice, but for years, I would go to whatever yoga class happened to be on offer somewhere easy to get to. No matter which class I chose, yin or ashtanga or generic community-hall-basement, balance was a problem. The instructor's announcement that we'd begin a sequence of standing poses always set off flutters of nervousness. I'd have visions of myself tipping over (which happened more than once) and knocking everyone else over in a cascade of yogic dominoes (which never happened).

Perhaps because I found standing balance hard to achieve, I was excruciatingly aware of the efforts that went into the attempt to achieve it. Two standing poses in particular, tree pose (vrksasana) and eagle pose (garudasana), were staples of these classes. Both poses require balancing on one foot with the other foot looped or braced against the supporting leg. I could hold these poses for only a few seconds, and for every single one of those seconds I was aware of the sole of the standing foot, pressed against a surface that did not present itself as solid and secure. In those moments, the ground beneath me became a quietly heaving mass of gravitational pulls and leans that eventually, always, toppled me over. I could feel these imbalances travelling around the edge of my foot, from the outer side to the softer inner boundary, and I silently chased them with what the teacher called *micro-corrections*: shifting a little bit this way, a little bit the other way. The instabilities and the corrections would then travel up the standing leg, perhaps following some bodily energy channel, setting off tremblings up and down my vertical self.

All of this was nearly invisible to the observer, as I found out when practising in front of a mirror. I couldn't see myself move in tree pose or eagle pose. The tilts of gravity under my feet, the efforts to regain stillness that filled my sensory awareness, appeared in the mirror as an occasional minor twitch.

Zoom out from the mat to the rest of life. My thirties and forties were the biographical equivalent of being stuck too long in tree pose. There were seismic changes in my world of work and relationships, shifts of gravity and weight that had the potential to knock me over, but they did not disturb the outward appearance of a more or less smooth passage through midlife. Not much, I think, was visible to anyone observing the pose, except for the therapist I saw semi-regularly. Some of the more dramatic destabilizations were apparent to the world—divorce, ex-spouse death, parental death—but in general I've continued to hold the pose for over twenty years without obvious teetering. The micro-corrections must be working, must they not? It looks like my stance is pretty solid. I don't appear unstable. But I have always been unbalanced.

In younger adulthood, feeling "unbalanced" meant feeling like I might disintegrate because of everything that was unsteady beneath the surface of my skin. For the first few decades of my adult life, that unsteadiness was a turbulent sadness that overlapped with depression, but was not reducible to it. I spent an extraordinary amount of time and energy looking for ways to change my thoughts or my actions, in order to defend against the miasmic melancholy that weighted my steps. I was fortunate that I managed to find those ways—therapy, church, exercise, antidepressants—and they kept me from going under while I accomplished most of the markers of successful adulthood, like partnering, parenting, and finding a profession.

However, what unbalances me now is not sadness or melancholy. It's rage. In the past several years, coinciding with Trump's 2016 election and the COVID pandemic and the acceleration of the climate crisis, the focus of my self-disciplining efforts has slipped sideways. Instead of defending against depression, I find myself constantly defending against anger, which seems to have infinite wells overflowing around me, like the biggest oil strike in history. While depression seemed to come from within, anger comes from the outside world: from small and large betrayals, from corruption and stupidity on the parts of leaders, and from witnessing what looks to me like apathy on the part of those who are led (a group that, if I am honest, includes me). I have not yet had to wrestle as intensely with other emotional demons like greed or fear—I'm in the country of anger.

Unlike melancholy, which, for me, involved almost obsessive inner vision, anger feels literally like out-rage—the problem is *out there*, the rage is against the wrongness in the world outside my head. In this respect, it's much better to be angry and out-raged than to be in-raged. It would be far worse to turn the anger inward and become melancholic or depressed. But my anger doesn't always tell me the truth (no, my sewing machine is *not* possessed by malicious spirits, no, the dog walkers in the park are *not* all clueless rich people), and it doesn't always let me see the world clearly.

I'm not alone in this. When I chat with friends around my age, conversations always seem to loop around to anger. One friend's boss embezzled a small fortune and let the company crash and burn in a furnace of debt. Another friend's parents are militantly, passionately, opposed to vaccination and her email inbox keeps filling up with the anti-vax newsletters they've subscribed her to. Another friend nearly underwent an unnecessary major surgery that could have compromised her vision permanently, because a physician forgot to make an appropriate note in her chart. It's not like we don't have reasons to be angry.

But the management of anger, even righteous anger, takes up a lot of bandwidth. What do you do for it? Thirty minutes of aerobic exercise three times a week? Read the latest book by Pema Chodron? Follow an anti-inflammatory diet? Anger is a curse we're saddled with, the curse of some malevolent fairy who visited our cradles at birth, and we work hard at dispelling it.

We weren't like this in our twenties, or even our thirties. What changed? It might be the sheer accumulation of years and the cumulative weight of things that have vexed us, made us irate, infuriated us (so many words for anger!). It might also be self-knowledge, and an attendant concern with self-care—not the scented-candles-and-fuzzy-sweaters kind, but the maintaining-sanity kind. We've all been through enough life to know that anger can be corrosive and toxic. It can knock you flat. It can also be a truth-teller. The trick is to stay balanced.

Like standing pose, middle age is a constant work of shifting and changing, paying attention to gravity. The world moves under my feet, but I keep moving too; the pose is never perfected, but neither does it fail.

Rowley

ROWLEY USED TO BE A THRIVING RAILWAY STOP, now it's a sort of professional ruin. Like many small Alberta settlements, it began with the trains, which started running in 1911 to bring coal from the Red Deer River valley to Calgary. Rowley's population topped out at several hundred in the 1920s. By the 1970s, the coal mines were gone, and by the 1990s, the train was gone too.

When the trains stopped running and the young people moved away, the remaining inhabitants of Rowley realized they had a choice. They could wither into nothing, or they could market their town's decrepitude as a backdrop for movies, a ready-made stage set. The hamlet is situated on a rise above coulees, looking out over a sea of flat land, primed for drama when the sun or the moon is high and the light hits the broad main street just so. The saloon, the general store, the grain elevators—Rowley is a western ghost town in drag as a western ghost town. I am almost certain I saw Rowley's present-day main street in the video for a gospel song by Tom Jones, with Sir Tom in a long black coat gazing out over the uninhabited coulee and some sort of filter applied to the images to make them look like a moving daguerreotype, brown and cracked and flickering.

My partner and I passed through Rowley in the fall of 2021. There are still a few well-maintained wood-frame homes in town, as well as a community mailbox where local farmers pick up their mail. There's a deserted church and garage and train station. There's a big square residence with flaking blue paint that looks like a boarding house, but it

< *Former business in the ghost town of Rowley, Alberta.* (*Photo by the author.*)

was actually a short-lived hospital. I imagined injured farmers, unable to get to Red Deer or Stettler for treatment, and rows of white-sheeted beds for the rural victims of the Spanish flu.

Someone had posted a notice on the old hotel saying that the monthly community pizza dinners had been indefinitely suspended because of COVID. The community mailbox and the COVID notice and the few well-tended, inhabited homes complicated the distinction between live town and ghost town, between the life and the afterlife of Rowley as a human community. These reminders of Rowley's unseen population were more ghostly than the abandoned parts of the town itself.

If the human inhabitation of Rowley was mysterious and a bit uncanny, the non-human or more-than-human world around it was abundantly alive. It was November, and we met flocks of geese on their southward migration, just before sunset. They billowed up from the ground: thousands upon thousands upon thousands of white birds against the mowed-over brown of late-fall fields, spotted with muddy puddles. The birds were talking, talking, talking in a rising and falling chorus of honks and calls. We approached, but we were in a car, not on foot, and the birds rose up through the noise. They took off in tranches, one white curtain rising, then another one behind it, then another one behind that. The honks and calls crescendoed as they lifted. They spun in the evening light with glittering white wings. From the underside, their shadows were dark grey. They were snow geese, I believe, with the odd Canada goose mixed in.

I don't think I've ever seen so many birds at once, undulating like a sea of white foam (and indeed this land was once a sea—we were in the basin of an ancient ocean that covered southern Alberta in the Precambrian era). If these geese had been birds of prey, they would have been terrifying. Even knowing that they are not birds of prey, being surrounded by so many alien avian intelligences, or perhaps one great avian intelligence, was disturbing and thrilling in equal measure. They moved into the air and settled back down, an enormous beating heart of birds slowing its rhythm, and we drove back to the main road and onwards to Drumheller to spend the night.

"Your Cell Will Teach You"

IN 2021, a friend of mine went to England to do research in a specialized archive and, upon landing at Heathrow, tested positive for COVID-19. This meant ten days of isolation in a hotel room at the airport, while her window of opportunity to see the archives slowly closed from ten days to zero. She is of a theological bent, and in a group email she recalled the words of the desert father Abba Moses: "Go, sit in your cell, and your cell will teach you everything." Her cell was a mid-range London hotel room for a week and a half.

I envy that cast of mind, that ability to turn an involuntary enclosure into a hermitage. The possibility of being fixed in place, of being enclosed when I don't want to be, is present in my consciousness now in ways that it never was before the COVID pandemic.

By early 2022, the pandemic was in its fifth wave. It looked like another long winter of isolation was ahead of us, another hermit-ish season. I recall thinking that this hermit-turn was both a privilege—in that I could choose to work from home and not be around people— and a burden, as there was no other choice that I could have made, and isolation is not a good way for me to live. The long, dark, and very cold winters in northern Alberta accelerated the sense of retreat, of withdrawal.

Withdrawal from the world has a long history. Most religions have some form of eremitical tradition. In Christianity, the earliest such retreatants were the group known as the desert fathers and mothers, who were active in the third century CE, in the area around Egypt. These monks and nuns left the urban life of the ancient Middle East, where Christianity had recently become first legal and then dominant, in order to find solitude and austerity. Their sojourn in the desert was understood theologically as a sort of long slow sacrifice, at a time when the quicker and more violent self-sacrifice of martyrdom was becoming a memory.

The stories of the desert mothers and fathers that have come down to the twenty-first century sound fantastical (but then, a few years ago, a worldwide plague shutting down cities in wave after wave of virus would have sounded fantastical too). When they weren't meditating on top of pillars or conversing with lions, they might walk for days or weeks to the hermitage of a fellow eremite, to give or receive pieces of cryptic, apophthegmatic advice. That advice is preserved in a book titled *The Sayings of the Desert Fathers*, which includes counsel about bursting into flame or hammering oneself like a lump of iron, as well as less esoteric information.

Many of the sayings in the book concern solitude and its virtues. One of the most famous is attributed to Abba Moses, who is also known as Moses the Ethiopian, Moses the Black, and Moses the Strong. He had been first a slave and then an expert thief before he turned to the desert. Moses's unsettled life before he became a monk meant that younger monks came to him for advice about how to reconcile themselves to solitude and quiet. "Go, sit in your cell, and your cell will teach you everything," said Moses to one such restless hermit. That advice—stay where you are and be filled with whatever is in that place—resonates through the long western European traditions of hermits, religious and otherwise.

Just before the great withdrawals of COVID began, I started to notice that hermits and solitaries of all sorts were having a bit of a cultural moment in North America. Solitaries like Emily Dickinson, Thomas Merton, and Julian of Norwich have passed into the canon of inspirational quotes on Instagram, and their visages appear on coffee mugs and Facebook GIFS. The idea of solitude was, in 2019, on-trend. Being alone in a simple place, regardless of one's spiritual beliefs, had an intuitive appeal for people like me, who felt oversocialized and somewhat melodramatically trapped by the jacked-up sensorium of a technology-enhanced social life that never seemed to slow down (until the pandemic came along, and the whole sensorium dragged or crashed to a stop).

One of the most popular revived solitaries is Julian of Norwich, who is known for calling out from her anchorage—a room cut into the wall of a fourteenth-century English church—that "All shall be well, and all shall be well, and all manner of things shall be well." Almost nothing is known about her life, not even her real name. She may have been a nun before she took to her cell sometime before 1395, or she may have been a widow and the mother of children who died. She may have had a cat walled up with her for company.

Her words, the assurance that all will be well, used to bring me a momentary rush of calm, but they don't anymore. In the self-pitying and petulant way that has become so distressingly familiar in this era of global crises, I think, *Well, it's fine for Julian to say all things shall be well—she chose to wall herself up in the church and spend her life writing poetry and mystical theology.* But I, in the midst of a lingering pandemic and a climate crisis and a war in Europe, can't expect that all manner of things shall be well.

This is a very twenty-first-century sentiment on my part, this idea that all things will certainly not be well, just because things are happening that threaten *my* health or *my* desired way of living. I am putting my own well-being in the centre of the cosmos, and by doing so, I am marking myself as someone whose worldview comes out of the post-Enlightenment European tradition, in which humans, with our needs and desires, are at the centre of the cosmos. The idea that my self-contentment is required for "being well," or that my own well-being is the measure of all things being well, would not have made sense in Julian's day.

The medieval anchorites lived in a death-saturated world, to an extent that seems morbid by modern standards of mental health. Julian would have entered her cell to the echoes of the Office of the Dead, a prayer cycle that was recited at funerals. The *Ancrene Wisse*, a thirteenth-century handbook for female recluses, recommended that anchorites practice digging their own graves within their enclosures, and that they not eat meals with the people who had sought their counsel—because while the dead may sometimes speak to the living, they should not eat with them.

(But this spiritual death could also preserve life. According to a 2008 biography by Elizabeth Obbard, Julian may have been able to survive the plagues that swept through fourteenth-century Norwich because she had almost no physical contact with other people—although she was revered as a source of wisdom and consulted with many people through a small window in the wall of her cell. In addition, Julian and other female anchorites would have avoided death in childbirth, which picked off many of the most brilliant female minds of the era. So their proximity to death, their embeddedness in death, may have saved their lives).

According to Julian's biographers, she entered her cell willingly and even joyously. This was not true for all anchorites. Enclosure could be involuntary, a cell could also be a prison, and separation from the world might not bring peace. This may have been the experience of an earlier medieval theologian, also enjoying a wave of popularity: Hildegard of Bingen.

Although Hildegard is now remembered as a polymath and radical visionary, she began her religious life as an anchorite when she was possibly eight years old, near the very beginning of the twelfth century. The period of her enclosure lasted somewhere between a third and a half of her life (no one is sure when she was born), but popular biographies tend to focus on the years after she left her cell, when her books and music and wise counsel propelled her into the theological and ecclesiastical history of late medieval Germany.

The young Hildegard was placed in an anchorage in Disibodenberg, Germany, under the constant watch and tutelage of Jutta von Sponheim, a slightly older girl from a family of minor nobility. Jutta was an extreme ascetic and penitent, who was walled into the same tiny room in the Benedictine monastery as Hildegard, most likely in a kind of double interment. Accounts of Jutta's life say that she had suffered a deathly illness as a young child and had promised to devote herself to religion if she recovered. But instead of becoming a conventional nun, she chose, or had chosen for her, the life of an anchorite. Hildegard was given to her as a companion. (I should note that most of my information about Jutta comes from Mary Sharratt's fictionalization of Hildegard's life—accounts from more mainstream Catholic sources are more generous to Jutta, often describing her as a mentor or spiritual mother to Hildegard. She was beatified as the Blessed Jutta of Disibodenberg.)

Hildegard (perhaps along with one or two other girls) was consecrated as "dead to the world" through a burial ceremony before entering the enclosure, which appears to have been one room with a small courtyard. Food was passed in to Jutta and Hildegard, and their wastes were taken out. The girls occupied the enclosure for decades, drawing an admiring following of local devout women with whom they were permitted to converse, but rubbing shoulders only with each other and the Benedictine monk Volmar, who was appointed to be their confessor. Either Jutta or Volmar may have taught Hildegard to read. Jutta and Hildegard remained in the cell until 1136 when Jutta died, possibly from self-starvation.

After Jutta's death, Hildegard, still behind the wall, came into her own. She was confirmed as abbess of the community of women that had sprung up in Disibodenberg, and then left her enclosure to lead the women away to start a new religious community (with financial support from Jutta's brother) when the paternal rule of the Benedictine monks became too confining, both metaphorically and literally. She wrote treatises on theology, music, medicine, and natural history. She argued with bishops and advised popes on political matters.

All of Hildegard's early years were eclipsed by this burst of accomplishments, eclipsed by the life that she stepped into when she left the cell in her late thirties. By the standards of the day, she was more than middle-aged. Being walled up had spared her from the dangers of pregnancy and childbirth, and may have helped her avoid infectious disease. When she emerged, she still had decades ahead of her before she died at roughly the age of eighty—a long life even by twenty-first-century standards.

I had been interested in Hildegard and known the vague outlines of her life for years, but realized only recently that somewhere close to half of that life was spent behind walls, with Jutta as her only companion, Jutta who does not seem to have been well at all. Year following year of immurement and seclusion—it could have been a near-lethal monotony with no discernible end, like a living death, or it could have been the seedbed of new ideas, new thoughts, and new religion that sprang forth when Hildegard was finally released.

How did she understand those years, as she was living through them? Did she see her life in the cell as sequestration until physical death, in the manner of Jutta, or as a time to gather one's forces and one's strengths, to prepare for what lay outside the only world she had known?

At the height of the pandemic, I was not immured, but neither was I totally free. If I had a cell, it was the size of Edmonton, or Alberta, or Canada, not the size of a couple of indoor rooms, and I had reason to think I wouldn't be stuck in that metaphorical cell forever. The pandemic brought isolation, but the people I saw through the windows on my laptop screen could be summoned at will for all sorts of reasons, work-related and otherwise, and I wasn't dependent on their alms. Yet despite all these differences and the intervening centuries, the stories of the anchorites, Julian and Jutta and Hildegard, had a hold on me.

I was in a mixed state of mind back then, with Jutta and Hildegard contesting for a place as the guardian spirit of pandemic isolation. On the good days, I felt like Hildegard, having new thoughts and learning new things and preparing (as I imagine she did, but I could be wrong) for a world that was waiting for my gifts. With that mindset, I could take the seclusion of the pandemic and hammer it into my own purpose, like the desert fathers and mothers who saw themselves as iron awaiting the forge. On the bad days, however, I felt like Jutta, at least the version of Jutta in Sharratt's book—anxious, touchy, only partly successful at containing the anger turned inward, prone to extremes in order to ward off an unknown future.

The desire to learn what I can from the place I'm in is much keener now than it was when I was younger. I know that the number of new places for me to go is limited by the time I have left, and so I will have to learn whatever it is I'm going to learn, from wherever I am. I didn't consciously choose this place to be my home—Edmonton, Alberta—but it's become so.

But my home isn't staying steady under my feet. Instead, it's roiling from climate catastrophes, right-wing populism, and the slow burn of the virus. I can't help but think about the end times, that I might be seeing everything fall apart. Perhaps the plagues and wars and dangers of medieval Europe had a similar effect on the minds of the contemplatives and hermits of the day. Maybe it's not so surprising that they saturated themselves with the knowledge of death. Jutta and Julian and Hildegard had a sweep of history informed by Western Christianity, with a dose of apocalypticism; I have ecology and environmental science with a similar dose.

This unsteadiness of home for me is true in the literal sense, as permafrost thaws and ice melts and topographical features sink and blur. I have a photo from 2000, the year I arrived in Alberta: I'm high-fiving the camera beside a small concrete plinth bearing a wood-burned sign reading "2000." This sign indicated the extent of the Athabasca Glacier, the most accessible outcrop of the massive Columbia Icefield. In front of me, not visible in the picture, was a trail of other year markers indicating where the leading edge of the glacier had been in the past.

I searched the internet for recent pictures of that year marker. The 2000 marker is now surrounded by gravel and scuffed earth, disturbingly similar to the surface of the moon. The glacier is still visible off in the distance, for now. Glaciologists estimate that the edge of the Athabasca Glacier is retreating about five metres every year, in addition to the loss of vertical height. The glacier will most likely disappear completely between 2060 and 2100. At some point, the year markers will cease to serve any purpose other than measuring what's been lost.

Reports from Indigenous hunters in the Far North today say that the ice is getting thinner, the muskeg boggier. I don't sense this directly because I live in a city, so what's beneath my feet most of the time is wood or plastic or asphalt. But under the floor, under the street, under the substrate, the earth is slumping. Changes that once took hundreds or thousands of years are now happening within decades. Even if I stay in my cell and let it teach me, my world will be unrecognizable to me in the near future.

These distortions of land and place have their parallel in distortions of time. I have a visceral sense that the land should not be changing so fast, and that some sort of temporal order is being violated when ice edges race back towards the shrinking glacial body. Century wildfires, the kind that used to happen every hundred years, should not be happening on the regular, every summer. These disturbances of space and time make me anxious. It's as though I have some undefined nervous disorder that connects my psychic equilibrium to the climate.

As I get older, these changes occupy a smaller fraction of my life than they used to. It's taken about twenty years for the Athabasca Glacier to retreat a hundred metres. At my age, that's just over a third of my life. But if I were twenty-five, this would have been going on for almost my entire life.

Perhaps this is why older climate change activists, in my experience, express more shock at the rapidity with which Earth is being burned up. In such a short part of our lives, so much has happened! By contrast, the younger ones have no less sense of urgency (after all, they're going to inherit this mess). But I don't hear the same note of incredulity, of having to force themselves to believe this is all really happening because it, whatever "it" is, didn't use to be this way.

From my vantage point, England in the fourteenth century appears a terrifying place, full of portents of a world coming to an end. Julian's kin would have been recovering slowly from the Great Famine of 1315 to 1317 and living through wave after wave of plague. They may have known that their king was at war with France in the Hundred Years War; they may even have known about the Great Schism that split the Catholic Church into factions with contesting popes. The Little Ice

Age was beginning, although no one called it that yet, which would disrupt agriculture and social life for centuries. But what about Julian herself—how much did she know of all this? Was she attracted or repulsed by the world outside her cell?

Two centuries earlier, in 1156, Hildegard stepped out into a medieval Germany that seems a bit calmer than fourteenth-century England. In her day, the Holy Roman Empire was still strong, expanding gradually to encompass Eastern and Western lands, ruled by emperors and lesser nobility who patronized the Church and sought the favour of monastic communities such as hers. The great plagues and famines of Europe were in hiatus and the Little Ice Age lay two centuries in the future. Hildegard would not have known it, but the life expectancy of her contemporaries was probably longer than that of their great-great-grandchildren.

Did she recognize the world when she walked into it? Maybe nothing outside her cell looked like it did the last time she saw it, when she was immured decades earlier. Saplings might have grown into trees; new land might have been cleared to supply the monks and the eremites with food. The monastery at Disibodenberg might have added additional rooms to accommodate the women who came to the community when Jutta and Hildegard were inside, seeking Hildegard's leadership. Perhaps the times had changed since she went into that cell; perhaps she came out into a new world, one that was ready to receive her gifts. Or perhaps nothing had changed at all.

Newcastle Mine

TO GET TO WHAT REMAINS of the Newcastle Mine, I took Highway 838, the Dinosaur Trail. I bypassed the turnoff for the Royal Tyrrell Museum, where the paleontological history of south-central Alberta is on display for millions of visitors a year. The old mine shares a provincial park designation with the Tyrrell (both are part of the greater Midland Provincial Park), but that's about all the two sites share. The historical past that the mine represents is much closer to the present, but much less spectacular. It does not attract tourists from around the world.

It's difficult to know when I'm actually on the grounds of the old mine. The landscape is layers of flatness—flat ground, flat-topped boulders, and small flat plateaus of sandstone here and there, elevated perhaps a metre. It resembles a floodplain, and may indeed be one. Every hundred metres or so, I spot a fragment of metal, blackened and curled with rust and weather and what might have been fire. Some are lying on the ground, others are fixed into the ground, as though the sand and dried mud of the plain has grown up around them. Some of these fragments were once implements for getting coal out of the earth, but I can't figure out where, exactly, they fit into the apparatus of extraction. A few larger pieces were once machines, and I can identify one, using Google Images, as a coal cutter. The area around me looks like the aftermath of a quiet disaster, in which the mine has been wiped out, leaving odd bits of metal behind.

< *Metal artifact at the former Newcastle Mine site, Midland Provincial Park, south-central Alberta.* (Photo by the author.)

Around the debris of the old mine, whorls of orange and red lichen spread across some of the more shaded rocks like a film. The rocks' crevices hold bits of green and yellow. I look closer—cacti! In flower! Two nights ago there was a hard rain, and the water has already translated into quarter-sized yellow translucent flowers, their white pistils dusted with pollen. Cacti in a desert shouldn't surprise me, but these do. I associate cacti with American deserts, the Mojave or Death Valley, not with Canada. But the heat and the rocks and the harsh rainfall don't know the difference between the Alberta and the Montana side of the border, and so neither do the cacti. These hardy plants look out of place to me only because I have an irrational feeling that Canada is not where cacti should grow. At the same time, I know that the cacti have been here much longer than the scattered metal implements from the mine that gives this site its current name.

Scrambling over rocks, I suddenly come upon a pit filled with water. It's circular, maybe ten metres in diameter, and surrounded by the only greenery of any size for as far as I can see. If this weren't an old mine site, I'd call it an oasis. The pit must be human-made—I can't imagine what natural forces might create something this perfectly round. It must have filled up during the same rainfall that brought the cactus flowers. The water is opaque, uniformly beige, and absolutely still. Blackbirds and other birds I can't identify sing in the cattails that border it. Something about the water's stillness pushes me towards the desire to interrupt, and I don't resist the temptation to pick up a rock and throw it. The *plonk* of rock on water suggests that the pit is deep, and the ripples spread out unhindered to the very perimeter.

I wander around the site until I start to worry that I don't know where I'm going. There are no marked trails, and my feet don't leave imprints on the sandstone. I see coils of barbed wire that must have marked a fence at some point, but whether they indicate some kind of barrier or whether they're just defunct is not clear to me. From one of the small plateau heights, I can see my car near the entrance.

Before I leave, I bend down to scrape and pull at an oddly shaped embedded metal item, wanting it for a memento. The dry-packed earth doesn't give it up easily, and I end up emptying my water bottle on the ground to soften it so that I can wrench and jimmy the thing free. It's some sort of electrical insulator, I can tell, but beyond that, I can no more identify it than I could any of the dinosaur bones pulled from the earth nearby, now re-articulated in the Tyrrell Museum. These bits of debris baked into the packed dirt tell me that people passed this way not so very long ago, in terms of geological time, but what they were doing, and why they brought this item along, is lost.

Time Management

THE SUMMER AFTER MY FIRST YEAR AT UNIVERSITY, I worked as a sort of general helper in what would now be called the professional development or in-house education office of the big IBM plant in Don Mills, Ontario. One of my tasks was registering people for their in-service "learning experiences," or short courses, which they were required to take two or three times a year.

This was in the early 1980s. Some of the classes and workshops had arcane titles that I now recognize as being signs of the dawning of the internet (Local Area Networks: An Introduction), but the most popular course was always Time Management. Everyone knew that Time Management meant taking a day or two off from their regular jobs and listening to some productivity expert pontificate about how to get more done in the same amount of time. The course wasn't demanding, nor did it have much applicability to real life at work. It also did not provide workers with more time to manage, which is what they actually needed. I heard repeatedly, as a joke, that one of the best ways to improve your time management was to avoid Time Management short courses.

Forty years later, Time Management has become an academic and professional field unto itself, with its own literature, cognoscenti, and adherents. I hear people talking about productivity cults and productivity gurus, but "productivity" seems to mean just doing more things in smaller amounts of time, as though there were no irreducible external limits on how much an individual can get done if they just comport themselves accordingly. Our efficiency, according to these experts, has no hard stop, only the soft limitations of our own ignorance, to be remedied by better technologies and new disciplines of the self.

Even when I was younger, I found this productivity obsession a bit ridiculous. It seemed like too much of a capitulation to capitalism, this work of constantly and even enthusiastically making yourself into a labour-minimizing device. However, it wasn't until recently that it began to annoy me for another reason, which was that productivity and time management had, at their core, a denial of the finitude of time—even though there is not, and never will be, enough of it.

The older I get, the more I know that to be true. Oliver Burkeman's book on productivity and time management, *Four Thousand Weeks: Time Management for Mortals*, came as a welcome tonic. Burkeman puts the finitude of time and the certainty that there will not be enough at the front and centre of thinking about time and work, rather than treating time as something to be hacked, something that will give way and yield everything we want if we just get our techniques right. The knowledge that I will not do everything that I potentially could do is oddly comforting, as the time available for getting things done grows shorter.

Going from time management to death management is not that far a leap. I'm also reading Atul Gawande's book on death, *Being Mortal*, and imagining what the title would look like with unconventional punctuation. Being? Mortal. Being: Mortal. Being/Mortal.

It's all there, in two words. As mortal beings, our lives are limited, and to exist means to be always coming to an end of existence. I'm reminded of learning about Heidegger in an introductory philosophy class, about how *Being and Time*, his notoriously dense masterwork, might more accurately be called Being Is Time, because human existence, before it is anything else, is temporal. Our consciousness does not exist apart from the knowledge that consciousness is finite. We may rage against the dying of the light, but the light nevertheless dies and so do we.

This rage has generated astonishing works of art, as writers, singers, painters, musicians push against the bounds of mortality. But in my own life, I don't know if I have the capacity for that kind of mortality-rage, even though I'm plenty capable of maintaining a constant hum of anger. When it comes to mortality—mine and the world's—I wonder if a slow, intelligent grappling with finitude, rather than rage, would suit me better as I proceed westbound.

What should we do in the face of our knowledge that we and our world are both going to disappear? Lisa Wells, in *Believers: Making a Life at the End of the World*, says that it's always a question about legacy. What kind of person do I want to have been? That's a better question than "Did my life matter," because there is no point in the future from which that question can be truly and finally answered. But there will be people who know what kind of person I am, or was, or will have been.

It's one thing for me to acknowledge the inevitable end of myself; it's another thing to extend that knowledge to the end of the world. Can I grapple intelligently with the mortality of human habitation on Earth? If we can't slow down or stop the devastating transformations caused by climate change—and I believe we can't, not fast enough to avert the catastrophes—perhaps we should turn our attention to what it's like, right now, to live on a heating planet. Not just the short sharp shocks of once-in-a-century heat waves and hurricanes, but the slower movements, the winding down. I wonder what it would be like to look on the world, not with the frenzied or futile desire to preserve, but with the desire to eulogize, to say good things, to remember how it was and will no longer be. To exist between lament and farewell.

Abbotsford

IT'S NOVEMBER 2021. I'm sitting in a coffee shop in Edmonton reading about the flood disaster unfolding in British Columbia. Pundits are saying this could be the biggest natural disaster in settler Canadian history. Highways are washed out completely, and the time to fix them is being estimated in months, not days or weeks. Today, the city of Vancouver is, incredibly, an island, with no road or rail access to the rest of Canada. I always thought that if British Columbia were to be devastated, the cause would be earthquake or fire or maybe rising sea levels on the coast—I did not foresee heavy rain and mudslides taking out the infrastructure. (The fact that I can imagine several different and very plausible natural disasters afflicting Canada's largest western city, yet still be surprised by this one, tells me that things are indeed sliding in all directions, as Leonard Cohen would say.)

The epicentre of the floods appears to be Abbotsford. I was there a few years ago with my daughter, whose cheer team was attending a big North American competition. The cheer athletes and their moms stayed in two nondescript and nearly empty chain motels on either side of an arterial road buzzing with streaks of Fraser Valley commuters.

On warm-up day, when the teams were practising in the cavernous sportsplex that is the architectural vernacular of western towns, I decided to walk to what my phone told me was downtown Abbotsford. It took several tries to get across the arterial roads, but when I finally found my way onto a barely used railroad track leading to the centre

< View of Mill Lake Park, in the centre of Abbotsford, British Columbia. (Photo by the author.)

of the sprawl, I hit my stride and hiked the last few kilometres into Abbotsford. The rails were damp and rusty, and the small storehouses that lined the railbed had tendrils of mould spidering down their cracks.

Abbotsford was a town that had seen much better days. It did not give off the west-coast Pacific vibe of Vancouver. Instead, it reminded me of British Columbia's more northerly logging towns, like Prince George or Fort St. John. The better days of Abbotsford, like most of those towns, were bound to the long-vanished dream of railroads knitting the farmlands and the sawmills and the mines with the cities.

Contemporary Abbotsford has a trendy main street with coffee shops and a French bakery, plus a few lawyers' and accountants' offices that spread a few blocks to either side of a central intersection, halfway up a low hill. When I dropped back down onto the old railroad bed, however, I saw a different, older town, curled around the up-to-date Abbotsford like old smoke around a fire.

This old town was a religious place, evidenced not so much by churches as by the number of Christian-run thrift stores backing onto the railroad, and the plenitude of Christian fiction weighing down their bookshelves. The most devout people in Abbotsford today, in terms of numbers, are probably members of the Sikh communities of greater Vancouver. But the town itself has conservative Christian bones. This part of British Columbia, like the northeast where Alberta and British Columbia meet, or the south-central Alberta stretch of prairie around Red Deer, is fundamentalist country, where Calvinists coexist with American-flavoured charismatic megachurches.

The biggest Christian thrift store in Abbotsford, however, was the Mennonite Central Committee's operation. The MCC is not just another notch on the bible belt. MCC Mennonites are left-leaning pacifists with strong agrarian roots, and they've been in western Canada for over a hundred years. In my earlier days travelling in Africa, I found MCC international development projects had very good reputations for being well run, honest, and integrated into their communities.

I spent an hour poking around that thrift store. It was a warehouse of serviceable goods that doubled as a museum of mid-century farm life, its artifacts tagged to sell for a few dollars. I saw milking stools and homemade cupboards with open hutches for showing off the good china. For a moment, I contemplated buying a hundred-year-old sewing machine that folded down into its table, but couldn't fathom getting it back home on a plane. Then I followed the railbed back out to the highway and the pedestrian-defying traffic, to wait outside the Motel 6 for the shuttle bus that would drop off the young athletes at the end of their long day of practice.

| The Abbotsford I visited a few years ago would have looked very different in late 2021. That fall, after days of continuous rain, the Nooksack River in northern Washington state, which has emptied into Puget Sound for as long as anyone has been alive in the region, changed its course. Under the pressure of the waters it turned north, into Canada, following its own ancient riverbed. According to a story on Washington's NPR affiliate, geologists had known that this reversal was possible, and the Indigenous communities in the area may have histories of a time when the Nooksack turned away from the ocean and became a "ghost river."

In late November, the Nooksack swept over the towns and farms on the Sumas Prairie floodplain, including Abbotsford. Flooding destroyed homes and businesses, killed livestock by the thousand, and cut off lower British Columbia from the rest of the country. The trouble goes back to climate change, as almost all trouble does—the Nooksack receives snowmelt from Mount Baker in Washington state, and warmer temperatures mean that snow is melting at the same time as rain is falling. The rain came from an *atmospheric river*—an oddly poetic term that I have since added to my climate crisis vocabulary. Atmospheric rivers are the air currents that carry water vapour from tropical latitudes northward. When they pass over the land, especially if a mountain range or other landform is in their way, the rivers stall, the vapours condense, and it all pours down as torrential rain. These rivers in the sky dwarf their counterparts on the earth; their flow can be up to ten times that of the Mississippi River at its mouth.

So—the river on the earth changed direction and sought out its old pathways, and the river in the sky slowed and fell to earth. These are fantastical descriptions of crisis events. They sound almost like magic.

News reports from Abbotsford held other images of the fantastical—
the giant sturgeon that crossed the highway on currents of floodwater
and swam into the power station, rescued by local men who struggled
to hold the enormous fish still; the cows that followed the motorboats
leading them out of submerged pastures, some of them roped together.
Things that I would never have imagined possible are happening.

Keeping Time

I RECENTLY HEARD a CBC Radio interview with Canadian poet George Murray, who is just a few years younger than I am. The interview was about Murray's retrospective collection of poetry, *Problematica*, which spans twenty-five years. He spoke of his surprise—shock would be too strong a word—at realizing that he really had been around long enough, and had written enough, that a moment of retrospection spanning a career might be in order.

It feels like someone else wrote the earliest poems, he said, because they were written so long ago. As a young man, Murray was always pushing ahead into the future, living in acceleration towards a time that hadn't happened yet. But when he reached the half-century mark, he says, something changed. He started being present to his life, to his journey, instead of constantly looking to what was going to happen next.

There's a lot of math involved in aging. Quantitative questions take on an added significance when there are more years to conjure with, and when they're getting scarcer. *What is my life expectancy? How much longer have I got? What is the ratio of years ahead to years behind? How much of my life did I waste on that job, that belief about myself, that partner?*

Even when I'm not thinking about proportions and ratios, and am only considering numbers of years, those numbers are bigger than they used to be. I have friends I've known for forty-five years. Very soon I will have known them for half a century. Our collective Next Big Birthday is when we all turn sixty. I never used to be able to apply words like "half a century" or "sixtieth birthday" to myself or my peers.

For me, these numbers are wrapped up in my westboundedness. Once upon a time, I came to Edmonton, and then I'd lived there for five years. Then a decade. Then it was two decades. Then I had lived longer in Edmonton than anywhere else. Then I had lived twice as long in the west as I had ever lived anywhere else. Now it's three times as long (my previous records were set in Toronto and Montreal, both places I lived for what felt like ages at the time). Babies who were born after I moved to Alberta have grown up to be adults. Clothes that people were wearing unironically when I arrived in Alberta are now costumes for "dress the millennium" Halloween parties.

I don't see myself leaving anytime soon, so at some point I will have lived in Alberta four times as long as anywhere else, and then more and more, like an inverted Zeno's paradox in which my time spent in the west approaches, but does not ever equal, all of my life.

I heard another interview on the CBC, this time with Chad Orzel, author of *A Brief History of Timekeeping*. Orzel makes the point that our consciousness of time is mediated by our technologies for measuring it, whether they be the great henges of Britain or wristwatches or atomic clocks. All of these devices serve to divide, quantify, and make apparent this invisible, silent thing, or condition, or whatever it is that we call time. Time as a phenomenon is *sui generis*: there's nothing to compare it to or distinguish it from.

I wanted to hear Orzel talk about time as experience, but on the radio show he seemed more eager to talk about levers and fixed gears. I still don't really know how to talk about what it's like to be a being-in-time, which I would be even if all the watches in the world got lost, and all the clocks stopped dead.

Orzel did say, however, that of the many ways that different cultures have found to divide time—all based on what can be observed in the natural world—none of them divide cleanly and perfectly into the other. A twelve-month year made up of only twenty-eight-day lunar months would soon be decoupled from the changes in temperature and precipitation and light that we call seasons. A few days would need to be added here and there so that the March of one year resembles the March of twenty years hence, so we don't end up with blizzards in

July. (Well, we might end up with blizzards in July, but they will be the result of the havoc we are wreaking on the planet, not the imprecision of our calendars.)

There is no way of measuring time that is truly fractal, where smaller units fit precisely into larger ones. Our days will always be slightly out of sync with our years. Our moments do not add up perfectly to our histories.

Rochfort Bridge

NEAR THE HAMLET OF ROCHFORT BRIDGE stands one of the longest railway trestles in North America. It's a spindly confection of timber gone black with age and newer patches of steel, stretching out like an object lesson on convergence until it disappears into the horizon. It crosses the Paddle River, a short and unremarkable waterway, and Highway 43, the main route from Edmonton to the northwest of Alberta. The 2,400-foot trestle is seldom used by trains.

The bridge is in the part of Alberta known as "West of the Fifth"— a geographic designation referring to western Canada's fifth meridian. In the late nineteenth and early twentieth centuries, the fifth meridian was the unofficial marker of the settlers' western frontier. Today it's hard to find a meridian on a contemporary map, but West of the Fifth lives on in the names of law firms and pet crematoriums in the small towns where grasslands begin the transition to low pine forest, and in the names of events such as the West of the Fifth Rodeo and the West of the Fifth Winter Poker Run (a steeplechase with snowmobiles in which teams collect a single playing card at each of seven stops, and the team with the best hand wins).

In Alberta, West of the Fifth has become a way of shorthanding an affinity for frontier culture at the northern tip of cowboy country. As a denotation of a physical frontier, however, it's a lexical ruin. It no longer functions. That frontier, that meridian, no longer marks the divide between one place and another.

< *Railway trestle, just east of Rochfort Bridge, Alberta.* (Photo by Michel Figeat.)

West of the Fifth, as a cultural or economic designation, names the uneasy terrain where oil and gas extraction overlaps with older agricultural practices, namely farming and ranching. The farmer, the cowboy, and the roughneck form a trident of frontier masculinity that persists in Alberta—in the form of country music and bumper stickers and the political rhetoric of right-wing parties. But the branches of this trident don't coexist so easily in living communities. Until the early twenty-first century, the fast money to be made in resource extraction industries siphoned young men out of smaller agriculture-based towns, and today the toxic overspill of fracking and abandoned wells poisons the ground that farmers and ranchers depend on.

When I was hopping around the internet trying to understand the cultural significance of being West of the Fifth, I came across an article from the local paper in Rimbey. This town is a few hundred kilometres south of Rochfort Bridge, and is one of many communities that have been hollowed out by the flow of young people to the oil and gas fields of the north. Reminiscing about the near-past, a newspaper columnist wrote:

> If one were to use monetary terms as expressions of success, recent history would demand the conclusion that the oil and gas industry are paramount. The people of this region however are aware of three important factors. First, we do not use monetary terms as our ultimate expression of success. We use traditional Western family values, a sense of community and an unparalleled work ethic for self-identity. Secondly the oil and gas industries are most often run and serviced by people who go home after a hard day's work in the oil patch and feed their cows or perform some other agricultural chore. Thirdly, agricultural enterprise will be here long after our wealth of hydrocarbon reserves have been exhausted.

The diction of this Rimbey writer defending the agricultural life seemed oddly stately to my ears. It was as though the words had been plucked out of nineteenth-century disputes over the true nature of the settler west, about whether the true westerner was the stationary farmer or the peripatetic cowboy or oilman. West of the Fifth is contested domain, in the imaginations of its chroniclers. Is it the staging area for trips to the north? Or is it the repository of "traditional Western family values," imagined as permanent and salutary?

From the "traditional Western family values" hovering over West of the Fifth, to the very concrete marker of that community: returning to the Rochfort trestle itself. The structure is a marvel. It's not entirely abandoned—the odd freight train still goes through—but it possesses the allure of the abandoned railroad. The urge to walk from one end to the other along the wooden slats, with the tiny meandering Paddle River far below, visible through the timber crosshatching, is almost irresistible.

It's not entirely clear why this bridge exists. It seems too imposing for such a small river as the Paddle. This rail line was never heavily used—the tracks here jut off to the northeast, away from the busy farming areas off Highway 43.

The bridge might even be one of Alberta's early twentieth-century railroad follies, overbuilt for a boom that lasted only a few years. The Edmonton, Yukon and Pacific Railway, or EYPR, near my home in Edmonton, is one such folly. A historic plaque has designated it "the world's shortest railroad with the longest name." The Rochfort trestle was completed in 1914, as was the EYPR. This was one year after the 1913 land bubble had burst, which brought the early twentieth-century grandiosity of the west to a halt, until the first oil boom charged it up again. Many of the ruins of Alberta have a 1913 cornerstone.

The hamlet of Rochfort Bridge looks weary. According to the 2008 municipal census, there were seventy-one inhabitants. I imagine that the number hasn't risen since then. All the commercial buildings are shuttered or are only notionally open for business, such as an antique store with a peeling hand-painted sign propped on the front railing, but no visible shopkeepers. In 2017, the annual Heritage Day celebration was called off because there were no volunteers to staff the farming demonstrations, music performances, and parade.

The site is pretty enough, with gentle hills descending into the Paddle River valley. There's a trading post just off Highway 43 that prides itself on being the "home of the bridge burger." Like most trading posts in such towns, it has an eatery with a separate seniors menu—a tactful way to appeal to customers who can't afford the deluxe version, whether or not they are actually seniors. There are also, legitimately, a lot of seniors in these places, especially with the young men finding work in the oil patch and the young women leaving for university, where they fill up my classrooms.

In recent years, the area around Rochfort Bridge has been associated with tragedies. Mayerthorpe, the closest town of any size, is where four Mounties were shot and killed in 2005 by a disturbed local man who harboured an illegal chop shop, a marijuana grow-op, and a cache of weapons on his remote farm location. The shooter himself was killed; two other young men, who claimed they were intimidated by the shooter into supplying him with guns and transportation, were convicted. Fourteen years later, a house fire killed five people, two grandparents and three young grandchildren.

I was last there in 2018, and I had the sense that if I were to return to Rochfort Bridge a few years hence, there might be nothing left of the town at all, except for the magnificently extended bridge, smelling faintly of creosote, just a little bit east, over the tiny river.

Pigeons

IN SPRING 2019, pigeons began landing on my third-floor condo balcony, filling the space with coos and random feathers and offloading prodigious amounts of droppings. After a few weeks of preliminary fluttering, one pigeon found an old blue plant pot, built a nest, and laid two eggs.

Birds do not belong on my property. I learned this two years earlier when I received a wooden birdhouse as a gift and put it on the balcony, and was informed by email from the condo board that the housing or attraction of non-domestic animals was prohibited. A year later, the condo board hired a professional bird-dispersing service to wrap the drainpipes and gutters with bird spikes, belts of plastic with spear-points to prevent perching. The intent was to make the building a bird-proof fortress, but the pigeons managed to squeeze themselves between the spikes.

The pigeons on my balcony were illicit, as well as uninvited and unwelcome. Yet I didn't dispose of their nest in the most efficient way, which would have been to pick it up and toss it into the garbage. I let it be. I found myself not only tolerating the pigeons but harbouring a nest whence new pigeons would emerge. I felt like the townspeople in old western movies who supply information and food to the bandits, abetting outlaws right under the sheriff's nose.

I couldn't bring myself to break up the nest, but I also didn't want pigeon droppings everywhere. Trying to reconcile these contradictory wishes, I first attempted to drive off the birds with a technique from the internet involving a lattice of old CDs held together by twine, meant to spin and shine in the sun. The lattice tangled in on itself with the first strong wind, and the pigeons ignored the clumsy flapping thing. So instead of trying to get them to go away, I rigged up a sort of pigeon litter box, involving a large rubber boot tray and industrial-grade bin liners. The boot tray went under the spot with the greatest concentration of perches, and I switched out the bin liner every few days.

Why did I bother trying to accommodate those birds? Why didn't I ratchet up the pigeon war by calling in the same mercenaries who had done the initial balcony work, to harden my balcony as a target? One reason was that I thought it would be futile, given the pigeons' resistance to twirling CDs and claw-catching spikes, so I settled for harm reduction instead of eternal warfare.

Another reason, somewhat sentimental and gooey-Disney, was a sense of fellow-feeling with the mother pigeon, who was the most assiduous in bringing back sticks and twine and fashioning them into something nest-shaped. She seemed to be on her own—no sign of a father pigeon—and I couldn't help but note that we were both single mothers, we had young ones to prepare for the world, and neither of us had a lot of help. I imagined a sort of maternal sheen to the mother pigeon's feathered breast, but that was pure projection. That pigeon was no more likely to feel human emotions than the spider plants draping the sill of the windows through which I watched her. We had both followed some sort of imperative to reproduce our species, but I should not extrapolate shared emotions from that biological symmetry. Still, I kept checking on her, even though her presence on my balcony was dirty and unpleasant when not seen through maternal rose-tinted glasses, even though she was not a particularly appealing bird.

Out on the prairies, I occasionally see kestrels freewheeling like kites, or hawks dropping low and fast on the trail of a field mouse. Pigeons, not so much. They are urban birds; they know the overhangs and eaves and cramped building spaces the way other birds know the field and the forest. Pigeons move into cracks and crevices, bringing white smears of mess and sticky feathers. They un-domesticated my condo. They were not exactly wild, but they were not pets.

Pigeons are runty little birds, prone to fighting and to scattering and eating garbage, prone to getting into places and pooping everywhere. They're rats with wings. Up close, they are more beautiful than one would expect, but few people want to get that close to a pigeon. They are not symbols of noble human endeavour, like the eagle or the dove or the wild swan. They lack the intensity of their cousins the ravens or the curiosity of Edmonton's emblematic magpies. The hipster urban-bird trend that I've noted on social media has been all about the urban chicken, which evokes retro rustic sentiments, not the pigeon, which is arguably the quintessential city bird.

Pigeons are also surprising. From an online article titled "15 Incredible Facts about Pigeons," I learned that they can be taught to recognize up to fifty-eight distinct written words. The authors of the pigeon-word study stress that the pigeons cannot decode the words—they aren't reading them in the same way as a human would—nonetheless, the image of quasi-literate pigeons with brains utterly different from primates is an uncanny one. They should not know our words, but they do. They should not be on my balcony, infiltrating my human space, but they are.

Edmonton doesn't have the lush encroachments of green found in cities that are farther south and closer to sea level, like Montreal or Toronto. We do have the largest urban park space in North America, a poplar and dogwood ribbon twisting along the North Saskatchewan River. We have some feral nature—hares skitter across the campus where I work, and coyotes take the occasional pet out of back yards. Pigeons, however, don't flicker at the margins of urban spaces like these animals. They don't come out of the dark to prey on cats and dogs or to dig up your first tender garden vegetables before vanishing back into the shadows. They move in. They infest. They want your territory.

A friend also had pigeons nesting on her balcony and she sent me a cellphone video of the babies. They were scrawny but feisty little dinosaur-like creatures, gulping down a sort of ooze that the mother fed them from her own body, like tiny cannibals on liquid diets. The nest on my property showed no such activity. I began to fear that my mother pigeon would be disappointed, that her eggs would not be viable and she would continue to sit on them long after life had sputtered out.

Then one day I opened the balcony door, my cat got out, and the mother pigeon levitated right off the nest in a blur of feathers. There, now exposed, were two baby pigeons—not adorable like Snow White's bluebirds, but also not the vaguely reptilian bald things I had expected. They were cute, in an odd way, busy beaks in the air. They were part of the world now, their world of eavestroughs and garbage cans, and I believe I'm not reading too much into their beady eyes when I say they looked eager to know what would happen next.

While I was watching the pigeons on my balcony and sharing pigeon videos, wildfires in the north of the province burned out of control, part of the ongoing climate collapse. The winter had been too arid, the summer fire season had started too early, the thunderstorms that brought lightning had become more intense and frequent. Decades of vigorous fire suppression programs had been too successful, stopping the small fires that burned away dead and dried wood, allowing the tinder to build up year after year.

Wildfires have never been rare in the boreal forest north of Edmonton, but as the world's trees and tundra start to burn and the feedback loops of heat accelerate, drying and then scorching the forest, the fires are getting bigger. In the twenty-plus years I've lived here, there have been at least three once-in-a-century fires. The town of Slave Lake and the community of Fort McMurray were destroyed in 2011 and 2016, respectively, and in 2019 wildfires forced people in remote Métis communities to grab what they could and run. The birds and mammals of the north, deep in the burning forest, must have fled too.

A few weeks after the baby pigeons hatched, the winds shifted and heavy smoke descended on Edmonton, some three hundred kilometres south of where the fires raged. The sky turned orange and dark and bitter particles of soot clogged our throats and eyes. Comparisons to Ragnarök, Mordor, Sheol, the Eye of the World, abounded on social media. To me, Edmonton's sky looked like images of the Martian sky transmitted by the Mars rovers: permanently rust-coloured. (Within a year we would see images from Australia that would put the reddish skies of Alberta into perspective. Walls of flame hundreds of kilometres long, with no roof but fire.)

I knew the wildfires up north were bad. I knew that hundred-year fires should not be happening every year. But the fires were still far enough away that they were the stuff of media reports, not immediate experience. I could contemplate the destructive power of the fires and turn those thoughts over in my mind without feeling the heat of the flames. Air conditioning, sealed buildings, and underground parking bolstered the illusion that I was not really in the same world as the fires, not sustained by the same air and therefore in no danger.

When the smoke first moved into the city, however, I lost the illusion of distance. It filled the outdoors; it slipped through cracks and ducts and came inside. Fine particles of ash settled everywhere. I picked up a book from a desk at work and saw a book-shaped rectangle outlined in grime. The smoke was a miasma, thick and harsh and seemingly possessed of a mindless malevolence. The premier of Alberta cancelled an outdoor press conference about the lifting of restrictions on industrial pollution because the smoke was so oppressive, which was both ironic and frightening.

I worried over the pigeons. They were only babies yet. Would they survive? Could they breathe this smoke and live? Were they going to be casualties of the lethal human carelessness that turned the forests into kindling? Should I bring them inside, where the air is artificially filtered by air conditioning? Or would that be too much for them, would the shock of being indoors hurt them more than the smoke? (Or would that be too much for me, would I be crossing the line between making pests of pigeons and making pets?)

As it turned out, they survived. The morning after the worst smoke I looked through the glass panes of the balcony door with anxiety, wanting profoundly not to see dead birds. I saw two piles of scraggly feathers—first one moved, then the second. The pigeons had come through. They had gulped down baby-bird lungfuls of bitter air and emerged, if not unscathed, at least still alive.

Two weeks later, the baby pigeons had grown to the size of adults and wobbled off, rising vertically and shakily on new wings. I took advantage of the moment to reoccupy my balcony, throwing out the plant pot they had nested in, cleaning up copious amounts of pigeon droppings, and sluicing vinegar over the whole area because I had read on the internet that the fumes of vinegar are to pigeons as wildfire smoke is to me. I had invested time, hope, and worry in the pigeons, but I didn't want them in my home any longer than necessary. I wanted to set the terms of my coexistence with the wild world, to assert whatever bits of dominion that I could.

After I purged and rearranged my balcony, it stayed pristine for a week or two, but then the pigeons returned. There was nowhere for them to roost anymore, but they scrabbled onto neighbours' railings, hovered gawkily over my balcony, and hopped one-footedly amid the bird spikes. They drove my cat on the other side of the window to distraction, ignoring her as she hissed and yowled inaudibly behind the glass. They are not to be gotten rid of. I had dismantled their home and scattered their birthplace, but they remember, and they come back.

After a month or so, the wildfires in the north subsided. I checked the province's wildfire status website every few days, and by the end of August, most of the fires were deemed under control. The great exception was the smoulder of High Level, still dominating an unimaginably large area. But its smoke and ashes no longer filled my eyes or my sky, and it was easy to believe the fire was so far away that it was no longer worth thinking about, for now.

The fires will come back, and so will the heavy smoke. There will be days next year—probably more days than this year—when I will feel the effort of breathing and I will worry over the smaller creatures, the ones who may not be able to breathe at all. Next summer, the pigeons will be back too. I will be drawn back into the borderland between the human world and the wild world, between what we can tame and what we can only fear.

Palliser Triangle

IN 2021, the deep cold of winter came early. By the end of December, we had already experienced a week of minus-40-with-the-wind-chill, the exact temperature where the Celsius and Fahrenheit scales meet and cross, so it no longer matters what metric you use. Late December was the only time that my partner and I could both be off work. If we wanted to leave town for a few days, it would have to be during this cold snap. But along with the cold came the depths of the Omicron wave of COVID, which meant that the idea of getting on a plane for a weekend away seemed unwise, not to mention too expensive.

We got in the car and went south—to the endless flatland of the prairie, to an Airbnb in a small hamlet in the Rosebud River valley. The plan had been to hike along the abandoned railway beds, but the intense cold meant we couldn't manage more than a perfunctory quick walk to the hamlet crossroads and back, a distance of barely two hundred metres. So we drove. And drove. The car was a little box of warmth and colour, moving through the ice and the blinding whiteness of untouched snow.

The area west of the Saskatchewan border and south of the Red Deer River is not empty. It's filled with ghost houses, collapsing farm buildings, log cabins sagging under the weight of years more than the weight of snow, and huddles of sheds, their tarpaper peeling. This is the territory of big agriculture, so the fields were still being worked during the warmer months; the land itself was not quiescent. But once there had been many more farmers in the area, many more people,

< *Winter fields in the Rosebud River valley, central Alberta.* (Photo by the author.)

than there are today. We drove for hours on rod-straight range roads and township roads, gravel under the ice, passing only a couple of pickup trucks and four-wheel-drives.

These lands are sparsely occupied for a reason. We were driving through the Palliser Triangle, the enormous steppe of arid grassland that pushes west from Saskatchewan into Alberta. The edges of the Triangle are not obvious to the untutored eye, but since the nineteenth century the region has been defined as having a base on the 49th parallel that extends from 100 to 114 degrees west, and an apex at the 52nd parallel. Unlike more fertile lands to the north and east that were cleared of vegetation by settler farmers, the topography of the Triangle has not been substantially altered by the intensification of white settlement and white agriculture. For hundreds of years, the Blackfoot, the Sioux, and the Cree used the area for bison hunts, driving herds of the animals over cliffs into river valleys. The ground was covered by a mix of prairie grasses; trees and larger shrubs were kept at bay through the Indigenous practice of controlled burning, which left the land as a larder for the bison. When Irish explorer and map-maker John Palliser came along in the mid-nineteenth century, he thought that perhaps the outer edges of the Triangle could be farmed in the European manner, but concluded that the heart of the Triangle was infertile, useless desert.

However, the Triangle was also a politically inconvenient desert for the new Canadian government in the latter part of the nineteenth century. Without a white, British-descended population to anchor Canada's territorial claim in the area, the new country was vulnerable to American vagabonds and adventurers coming up through the long drylands stretching away to the south. In the 1840s and 1850s, restless Democrats in the United States used the slogan "54-40 or Fight!" to express a claim to the continent as far north as the 54th parallel (which would have put their border somewhere near present-day Edmonton). And so the Palliser Triangle was implicated in one of the most common political narratives of settler Canada—the question of how to keep the Americans out.

Palliser's assessment of the inner part of the Triangle as a barren wilderness was drowned out by nationalist politicians in Ottawa and in London, who saw an opportunity to fill up a potentially contested region with white settlers loyal to the Canadian and British flags. The prospect of a trans-Canadian railroad was also in the air, and indeed was a precondition for British Columbia to enter Confederation. If the railway went through the southern part of Alberta, rather than the more fertile northern part, it would not only link two sides of the country but would also keep American railroads from encroaching—and provide opportunities for settlements to be established along its path. And so the selling of the Palliser Triangle began.

The land rush was short-lived. Prospective farmers from eastern Canada and the British Isles, naïve to the west, were encouraged to buy up land near the railway, enticed with images of bumper wheat crops. They brought plows to break the soil, but it promptly dried up and blew away. A few American farmers, those with experience in dryland conditions in the Dakotas and the Great Plains, came north with their knowledge and skills, but not many lasted more than a few seasons before giving up and returning home. The Indigenous practices of maintaining the land through controlled burns and bison foraging were pushed aside, and the result was failure after failure. Towns came into being along the rail lines and bordering the riverbeds—Robsart, Loomis, Etzikom, Burdett, Lomond, Kinnondale—but most winked out after a few years, or, if well favoured with a school or a post office or a watering station for steam trains, a decade or two.

The 1920s and 1930s were the worst years in the Canadian dry belt, as they were in the American Plains states. The Canadian government created the Prairie Farm Rehabilitation Administration in 1935, which tried to keep settlers on the land through plans to build dugouts to hold water for cattle and to stabilize the soil by planting trees, but it was too late. In 1936 nearly fourteen thousand farms were listed as "abandoned" on the census. The title of David Jones's 1987 book about the Triangle sums it up: *Empire of Dust: Settling and Abandoning the Prairie Dry Belt.*

Today, big agriculture has taken over from smallholder farms scrabbling at the edge of viability. The Triangle is now home to large cattle operations, and the unmistakable brilliant yellow of canola overlaps with the more subdued hues of wheat and other grains, in fields that seem to go on forever. Even so, some of the early European settlers' descendants are still here—farm families with enormous sprayers and combines, and Mennonite colonies, whose neat complexes of buildings are set far back from the roads, looking like a cross between a small town and an army base.

Among the settlers who remained, who are still farming today, we see the marks of the dryland farmers, the old bones of what they left behind. Houses and sheds are stalled in mid-collapse, in an advanced state of decay. It's somehow fitting that this region is just a bit east of the main dinosaur fossil beds in Alberta, where the oldest of the old bones still come to the surface along the edges of the riverbeds.

In other parts of the province, abandoned farmscapes show a story of stepwise progress—the really small house, the slightly bigger house, the next house with a bit of ornamentation and a summer kitchen— but not so much here. The Palliser Triangle presents a panorama of abandonment that is bleaker, starker, with almost nothing to break up the line of sky at the horizon. Seeing this region in the depths of winter, with snowdrifts burying all signs of canola or wheat and only a few frost-rimed cattle crowded, unmoving, around their troughs, was like seeing an extraterrestrial planet-scape, where people had either only just arrived or had all disappeared.

That day, it was cold enough outside to kill you quickly. The brilliant blue of the sky—brilliant blue above brilliant white, in an atmosphere so frozen you could almost see the ice crystals in the air—added to the otherworldliness. This was a vision of the western sublime, alien and indifferent to settlers, yet also irrevocably marked by them.

Who Is That?

I'M CONSCIOUS OF CHANGES in my own embodiment as I get older, and not necessarily of the physical-decay kind. The aging of the body has so far been less eventful than I expected.

Nonetheless, I have changed, as an embodied person. I notice this not only when I look in the mirror and see who I am today, but also when I turn from the mirror and scroll through any form of social media that has my date of birth. As an aging woman on the internet, I'm hailed by the purveyors of technologies and practices intended to make the years go away. There's an entire industry out there that requires that we be brought face to face with the evidence of time passing—sagging skin, wrinkles, grey hair (or no hair), too much fat (or fat in the wrong places)—which can be smoothed away with the purchase of an elixir or a device or a session of intense pulsing lasers aimed at the "problem spots."

In addition to targeted advertising, I'm inundated with middle-aged memes and jokes and internet funnies about aging women. These veer from a desperate sprightliness, epitomized by the doggerel about the old woman who wears purple, to a sort of *opera buffa* depiction of the grotesqueries of menopause, played for laughs. I am quite righteously repelled on feminist grounds by the latter, but also put off by the former. I have no intention of joining the Red Hat Society, of being spunky or sassy in my remaining years.

I'm less interested in the physical alterations of aging than I am in the changes in social categories that accompany those alterations. One of those changes has to do with being seen, and with who sees us. It's a truism that older women become invisible in heterosexist societies when we're no longer considered as attractive to straight men as younger women. This is sometimes lamented and sometimes proclaimed as a triumph, as in Amy Schumer's "Last Fuckable Day" sketch, which I've shared and re-shared with middle-aged friends.

However, my experience is more subtle than just becoming invisible. Instead, I seem to have slipped out of the broad category of "young woman," and I'm now recognized as a "woman of a certain age," which could mean anywhere between forty and seventy. One middle-aged woman is pretty much like the next, and also, significantly and consequentially, pretty much like everybody's mom.

Here's a story. When I was in graduate school in the mid-1990s, I had a classmate named Barb. Barb was a second-career student—she had returned to school after raising kids, which meant she was about twenty years older than most of the rest of us, which meant she was slightly younger than I am now. Grad students earned pocket money by invigilating undergraduate exams, and so one day Barb and I were scheduled to oversee an Intro to Economics final. One student fell ill partway through the exam—the result of stress, food poisoning, or some virus getting loose in the dorms, maybe. He looked really green, so I called the paramedic. I asked the student if he wanted someone to accompany him to the hospital. "Her," he said, indicating Barb. "Can she come with me?" Baffled, I looked over at Barb. She whispered, "He wants his mom. His mom's not here, so he wants the person who looks like her." In my late twenties, I did not look like this student's mom. Perhaps Barb did.

Now that I'm older than Barb was then, I experience that look-at-me, see-a-mom resonance in my own encounters with younger adults— not so much in the direct encounters, when I talk to people, but in the near-misses or glancing encounters, when I think I see myself in someone's eyes, or when I find myself momentarily conscious of how I might appear to others. Sometimes I imagine that they see me as a maternal figure, but the more disconcerting moments are when I see myself that way. I am not only being written into the script as a mom,

I am writing myself into that script, in which every young adult is a stand-in for my actual or putative offspring.

Living in a university city, I not infrequently encounter loud or mildly obnoxious drunk young men on the street. I have never been especially liable to street intimidation, so my first reaction to the noisy youth yelling at his buddies has always been irritation rather than fear. In my fifties, however, this irritation takes on a different cast. My age means that I can see these twentysomethings as youngsters, who could have been children yesterday. *For Christ's sake*, I think, *I'm old enough to be your mother, buddy. You're not that much older than my kid.* And as time goes by, my kid gets older and so my parental proximity to the roistering youth becomes more and more plausible.

If I were being completely objective and rational, my age or generation compared with the university students taking their parties to the street shouldn't have any relevance to my judgment of their behaviour. Obnoxiousness on the street is obnoxious, no matter what the age of the miscreant relative to me. But still, the phrase rises up unbidden: *I could be your mom, for crying out loud!*

This generational identification is not thwarted by visual cues that indicate that I may be an unlikely candidate for a particular person's mom—when the obnoxious youth has skin of a different colour from my own, or has other markers of an apparent ethnicity that is not my own European whiteness. I still experience the pull of that generational self, even when it's physiologically or genetically unlikely that I could be that person's parent.

It's not really about the specificities of my encounters with these strangers, it's about me seeing myself, and about how old I perceive myself to be in the world—older-than-your-mom, old enough that I see you at a remove of several generations, you yahoo in the street. Would your mom approve of you breaking a beer bottle against the doorstep of the Commercial Hotel? I can assure you that she would not.

Most of the time, my recognition of change takes a less irritable, more quizzical tone. Like many people, I see my reflection and I think, *That can't be me*, while I know very well that it is. The doubleness is ambiguous, perplexing. That person in the mirror has too many years behind them to be me. That person has been around for longer than I have.

Recently, however, I've started recognizing the person in the mirror. I don't mean that I see myself, who I've been since birth. Instead, I see my maternal grandmother, or someone who looks like a slightly filtered version of her. I seem to have skipped over identification with my mother and gone directly to the first person that I ever knew to be an "older woman," the first person who inhabited that category in my mind.

My grandmother in her fifties was a handsome woman of the no-nonsense sort. Brilliant white hair, unfashionably short where mine is unfashionably long, creases of skin setting off high cheekbones and brows. She could have been mistaken for a peasant or a female don at Oxbridge in the 1920s (but was neither; she was a high school teacher in Kingston, Ontario). Seeing her return in my face could be a bit uncanny, but as I liked my grandmother and was often told that I was just like her, it is entirely canny, and I can feel the pieces of my history fitting into my present with a mental *click*. The wheel is turning. I am coming into the place of my ancestors.

Bunchberry Meadows

I SPEND A LOT OF TIME WALKING, and my favourite trails are at Bunchberry Meadows Conservation Area, in Parkland County. The trails have a lot of ups and downs, which means, I think, that I am technically hiking, not walking, but no matter. The conservation area is part of the Devon Dunes, an atypically sandy area that came into being after the last glacier passed through. The combination of sandy soil with low-lying marshy areas and steep inclines probably made this particular tract of land less attractive for farming than the land surrounding it, just outside the western edge of Edmonton, bordering the Enoch Cree Nation.

The name of this conservation area dissuaded me from exploring it for years—"bunchberry" sounded far too cute, like a Disney version of the pastoral, and I've come to associate anything called "meadows" with sprawling subdivisions that are not remotely meadowlike. But a bunchberry is a type of small dogwood, the most prolific shrub in Alberta, and meadows are indeed part of this native parkland, so the name works after all.

In addition to disliking cute names, I also dislike referring to anywhere as my "happy place." But if I did use that term, Bunchberry Meadows would fit. The Aspen Parkland trail cuts through hills and fields and wetland, with magnificent groves at either end. One grove, about a

< Abandoned car found in the Bunchberry Meadows Conservation Area, near Edmonton, Alberta. (Photo by the author.)

kilometre south from the beginning of the trail, is birch (rare in Alberta, where birches are almost always mixed in with other trees, especially their poplar cousins) and the other grove, about fifteen hundred metres from the end as the trail loops back to the parking lot, is golden tamarack, where the needles underfoot are so abundant and so soft in the summer that the word *carpet* comes to mind.

Passing through these groves is like walking through cathedrals— small cathedrals, to be sure, not Notre-Dame or Chartres, but semi-enclosed spaces, almost silent, where the light and air are filtered through living pillars. They remind me of the green-charged landscapes of fantastic novels, the forests of Narnia or the mountains and fields of Earthsea.

The property has its ruins, too. About a kilometre from the end of the Aspen Parkland trail, you traverse a meadow with gentle ups and downs. Off to the side, partially hidden by a screen of spruce, lie the remains of an old car, probably dating from the 1940s. It's been there long enough that it has sunk into the soft matting of the forest floor, so the wheel wells are half-buried, and the passenger-side door is permanently wedged open. In a wetter climate this vehicle would be rusted out to a skeleton, but Alberta is dry enough that the frame is still largely solid, if not intact. It's just listing downwards, not drowning. The car's wires and ornamentation have been stripped away, most likely by human scavengers, and the seat upholstery has been pecked or chewed off, probably by a generation of mice or birds long dead. A chrome door handle and the remnants of a hood grille are incongruously bright; the rest of the hulk is mottled black.

Over the years, I've noticed that the car is almost irresistible to kids. Every summer there's a worn path through the vetch groundcover, leading down the slope to where the car came to its final rest. It's a benign ruin. There's no danger for small children to explore— nothing about this vehicle moves anymore, and it has no sharp edges or deep holes. The years that have blended it into the forest have also neutralized it as an object of power.

One summer I encountered grandparents whose young grandkids were clambering around the car. We chatted, speculating on how it might have ended up there. There are no signs of a crash or an accident.

There are also no remains of any dwellings in the immediate vicinity, where the car might have been parked before it was abandoned. One theory: the path through the meadow is wide enough that it might once have been a dirt road that could carry automobiles. There are also some working farms in the area, as you get closer to the town of Spruce Grove, although most of the former farm territory is now given over to suburbs. Was this hiking path once a motorist's shortcut between farms?

The grandmother opined that the car's demise may have been the result of a ditching, which happens in rural areas in deep winter, when snow piles up. The car could have skidded just a bit, slid off the road and into the ditch, if indeed this was a road, and ended up buried in the snow so deeply that it couldn't be dug out. The car looks like it came to a halt peacefully, with no evidence of impact or rolling. If this is what happened, the snow may have simply taken it in, cushioned its transition from moving vehicle to stable object. The driver (and passengers, if any) may have just walked out. There's a range road not that far away, and in the winter it would have been a passable route from the site to wherever help might have been available.

Late last fall, I went out to Bunchberry Meadows for a last hike before the snow. I passed through the birch cathedral and the tamarack cathedral, and glanced at the ruined car down in the ditch as I traversed the last upland meadow. Later, while driving home along rural roads at the edge of the city, I noticed another ruined car that I couldn't recall seeing before. It, too, was in a slight depression in the ground, surrounded by trees. Like the car back in Bunchberry, it looked about eighty years old, with a curving cleft hood and bulbous gaps where the headlights once were.

I had never registered the sight of it before because the trees had always been in leaf when I passed by, whether the vivid green of summer or the orange-and-yellow palette of autumn. But in late November, with the branches stripped bare in anticipation of the long cold, the remains of the abandoned car solidified into an object in my vision.

Top Ten Crises

IN HELEN MACDONALD'S COLLECTION OF ESSAYS, *Vesper Flights*, she writes about her experience of migraines. She starts to notice strange sensations before the migraine itself takes hold—distortions of perception, nothing disabling but many things odd. With years of experience, she learned to recognize these as a prodrome, a collection of signs that a migraine was on the way. Yet when in the grips of the migraine, she writes, she loses the ability to connect the prodromal dots, to put one thing beside another and recognize how they influence each other. The migraine appears to render its own precipitating conditions incoherent, to induce a kind of limited amnesia, or perhaps it's more like aphasia, specific to migraines. The migraine makes Macdonald an expert in denial, able to experience pain and yet not quite register what it means.

I get migraines too, though mine are not as debilitating as Macdonald's. For me, the warning signs of migraine are more straightforward: pain in the sinus cavity above my right eye, then worse pain, then pain radiating around the right temple, then pain spiking if I move my head or look towards a source of light. Changes in barometric pressure, air pollution, or psychological stress can bring it on. Sleep, darkness, and medication will take it off. I am comparatively lucky in my migraines.

The migraine-denial of the migraineur like Macdonald is different from the migraine-recognition of the migraineur like me, the here-it-comes-again acceptance. Macdonald connects her inability to recognize the migraine-in-the-making to the experience of denial, or refusal of the knowledge of climate change. The bad news keeps coming through, lighting up every form of media and every conduit of information, and yet there's something missing in our ability to grasp the big picture, the really big picture, the biggest picture of all, the picture of the world. Macdonald mentions that some scholars think human brains may not have been set up by evolution for the task of contemplating the end of the world. Our species has been preoccupied for hundreds of millennia with smaller and more local matters of survival, and we have not developed whatever it takes to comprehend such a complete and overwhelming threat.

This strikes a chord. The same experience of not being able to keep the information together, of not being able to understand the connection between the pain that is experienced and the source of that pain, arose for me at the end of 2021 when my email inbox filled up with end-of-year lists. From Bloomberg, CNN, *Scientific American*, the *New York Times*, and other mainstream sources came compendia of the biggest climate stories of the year. The top ten environmental stories, the five biggest climate articles, the fifteen most-read climate crisis "explainers." Heat and wildfires, Biden renewing oil and gas drilling leases, COP26 in Glasgow, the first rain ever recorded in Greenland, floods, floods, and floods.

I wanted to organize this information, to make sense of it. *The floods in Henan are killing people directly but the rain in Greenland isn't however its existence signifies another step into the Anthropocene or is it the sixth great extinction or maybe both but the US has rejoined the Paris Accord but that won't stop the Sahara creeping north and the soil blowing away so we need Extinction Rebellion.* It all fits together somehow, bound with the glue of greed and short-sightedness, but I can't for the life of me lay it all out, diagram it so that the causes and the consequences become clear. I don't understand the assignment. It's like having an overwhelming migraine experience, feeling pain in all parts of the body, attention ricocheting from head to lungs to fingers to bowels, yet being unable to form the thoughts: *This is a migraine, I am having a migraine. This is what a migraine feels like. I understand what is happening to me.*

The top ten climate crises differ from migraines in one important respect. Perhaps because I don't have the same dissociative aspect to my migraines that Macdonald does, the onslaught of information about climate change doesn't hit me with the same embodied and wordless force. It's a cerebral shock, not (quite, yet) a corporeal one. It's not the back of the brain, the lizard brain, that is shorting out because I can't take in this information, it's the reasoning, logic-assembling front part.

I have always been good at seeing connections, at building the chains of influence through which one thing causes another to happen. In one of my first classes in graduate school, we learned about the techniques of analysis and synthesis—analysis, breaking a phenomenon down into its constituents, and synthesis, putting parts together to form a whole. I could do both. I could take things apart—ideas, narratives, concepts, apparatuses—and put them back together.

But I seem unable to analyze or to synthesize when what's in front of me, the matter in question, is the possibility of the end of human life. This is not a paralysis from fear (or perhaps it's not *just* a paralysis from fear); it's a failure of reason. The mental connections I can make among other parts and other wholes escape me when the parts and the whole are bigger than anything I can imagine.

This is because climate change is what philosopher Tim Morton calls a *hyperobject*: a thing that is so large, so widely distributed, and so totalizing in its consequences that it is not just painful but impossible to grasp the whole of it. There is, in fact, nothing that is outside the "whole" of the hyperobject. The spatial distribution, the temporal scales involved, would require a mind very different from the one we've got to be able to comprehend them. We will never have all the information.

And perhaps we don't want all the information. The incomprehensibility of climate change may actually be the result of wilful incomprehension. Novelist Ben Okri, in a 2022 interview with the Buddhist magazine *Tricycle*, called this possibility a "fascinating problem":

We don't want to know. Yet that which we don't want to know is going to fall upon us if we don't know about it. So not wanting to know is hastening that very thing that we don't want to know about. Except that we will then know about it in a way which is much worse than being told about it.

This tension between knowing and not knowing, between being aware of what is coming down the pike and being incapable of awareness, echoes through the literary writing on climate change. Climate writers seem preoccupied with the existential state of nonexistence. The possibility of not being alive at all—a state in which not only do we not know about climate change, we cannot know about climate change—gets invoked repeatedly.

Daniel Sherrell's book *Warmth*, about his memories of trying to live on the warming planet, is addressed to his child, who is as yet unborn for most of the events the book covers. The unfathomable nonexistence of this phantom child, the second-person reader who is not real, counterpoints the very fathomable possibility of nonexistence for the entire world that Sherrell is writing about, the world that he is trying to preserve.

In *Learning to Die*, Robert Bringhurst and Jan Zwicky look at things from the other end of life's journey, when death rather than birth is the event separating those who exist from those who do not. They argue that we should conceptualize the climate crisis in terms of our own nonexistence; that the most salient fact facing people who are living through the Anthropocene is that we are going to die; and that beneath the details of all the component crises, what we are really dealing with is the imminence of our nonexistence. It appears to be impossible to talk about climate, beyond technical reports and data points, without talking about things that, almost by definition, defy language and conceptualization. Like nonexistence.

This may be why I, like many others, get my catastrophe information from dystopian fiction, why I rely on novels and stories and movies to tell me what is happening, even when they leave me in a migraine-like state. This means outsourcing my knowledge to writers and artists who may not be scientists, who may not be well informed, and who may in fact be making things up.

My bookshelves are getting full. There's *Clade*, there's *The Ministry for the Future*, there's *The Overstory* and *Bewilderment*, there's *The City in the Middle of the Night*, there's *American War*, there's *The Water Knife*. In 2016, literary critic Amitav Ghosh lamented that climate change, which was by then both obvious and frightening, had not made the mark it should have made in popular fiction; less than a decade later, this is no longer true.

This sort of stunned incoherence is not a problem that I've had with other apocalypses. I grew up in the last years of the Cold War and went to disarmament rallies when I was in high school. I knew how a nuclear bomb worked, knew the difference between an A-bomb and an H-bomb, knew what the uranium and heavy water were for. And, thanks to an earlier generation of dystopian literature, I knew what radiation did (or I thought I knew), how it destroyed living cells and changed genetic material.

More recently, because of my professional work, I needed to learn about apocalyptic viruses, specifically HIV and Ebola. I could explain what a retrovirus is, I could describe how hemorrhagic viruses destroy internal organs, and I knew the metrics and the abbreviations—viral loads, incubation periods, R-values, T-cells. This knowledge was reactivated with the advent of SARS-COV-2 in 2019, and my grasp of the information had held up quite well. I became a bit of a pundit on local media, explaining (and overexplaining) how pandemics work, what exponential growth means, the two stages of the human immune response, and why vaccines are effective. So it's not that I lack the capacity to understand complex information—even distressing complex information.

But nuclear war and pandemics are, for want of a better word, *simple* catastrophes in their destructive mechanisms. The political and economic contexts surrounding these catastrophes matter enormously, but the ways in which they hurt people are pretty straightforward. A nuclear bomb has a hypocentre and circles of impact spreading out from it. Viruses are dumb creatures and they do only one thing, which is to hijack living cells and force them to churn out more copies of viruses.

With the climate catastrophe, though, there's no centre, no single thing that keeps happening over and over with lethal effect. There's the huge shearing-off of ice sheets in the Antarctic, and the single polar bear stranded in Churchill, Manitoba. There's the advance of the mountain pine beetle in western Canada, and the depopulation of the Tigris–Euphrates valley. There's the despair of people swarming the beaches in Australia to get away from the wildfires, and climbing trees in Mozambique to escape the floods.

Some of the disasters are happening now, some will certainly happen within the next decade, and some might be avoided or attenuated, muffled, if a collective "we" acts decisively right away. But that probably won't happen. *Because no one will commit to cutting carbon emissions deeply enough because there's no viable substitute for fossil fuels yet although renewables are getting better all the time but not quickly enough to keep global heating to less than three degrees because the feedback loop of albedo and reflection is accelerating and...*

The pieces fall apart again in my mind, even though I try to connect them on the page.

Beaverhill Lake

WE DROVE TO BEAVERHILL LAKE in hopes of seeing some of the sandhill cranes that migrate south in the fall and break their journey near Tofield. They follow the North American Central Flyway, a vast invisible path in the sky that curves from the Yukon to the breeding grounds of southern Texas. Looking at pictures of the flocks, I'm reminded of the old Anglo-Saxon word for the ocean: the *whale-road*. These migrating birds and sea mammals have their own paths that dwarf our highways and gravel roads.

There are no hills anywhere near Beaverhill Lake, despite the name. The land is flat, flat, flat—stubbly golden-brown hayfields as far as anyone can see, intercut with the old railway and a few agrichemical plants. This area is a mini-topography within the surrounding aspen parkland, like a plateau spread within an aspen forest. We take the paved road to Tofield, and then rumble over gravel for the next ten kilometres to the lake.

The lake itself is also a great flatness. This is not unusual for prairie lakes, which tend to be wide, shallow, and silty, unlike the bracing depths of Canadian Shield lakes that I remember from summer camp in Ontario. At Beaverhill, several years of near-drought have disrupted the water supply, so the lake exists almost in name only. It might better be described as a marsh with deep spots. We can't actually see open water at all. Fields of cattails and rushes spread out, obscuring whatever remains of the lake at the centre. When I try to walk closer

< *Cattails and rushes at Beaverhill Lake, near Tofield, Alberta.* (Photo by the author.)

to catch a glimpse of water, my feet quickly sink into muck, releasing algal smells with each step. I don't want to lose a shoe—or worse, get immobilized in the mud—so I retreat to drier land.

There are definitely beavers in Beaverhill Lake. We don't see them, but we see their slipways—slick mud trails leading out of the marsh, channelling a slurry of silty water from the flat pan of the lake to the edges; rushes bent over and pushed down, thwacked by beaver tails and paws. The beaver trails lead to stands of young aspen, many of which have already gone into fuelling the beavers, judging by the distinctive pointy tooth marks. These are some large beavers, if the width of the paths means anything, with crushed plants fallen to either side.

When I see such a disruption of the landscape, I'm conditioned to assume there is a human intelligence behind it, to read human determination and intentionality into the scrapes and traces. I'm used to thinking of humans as the only animals who direct the flow of water and mud. The beaver trails look like an intricate system, like there should be a map somewhere explaining how to get from point A to point B. The sky might look that way to the cranes, crisscrossed with distinct pathways of air, invisible to the non-birds.

We don't see the cranes, or at least I don't think we do. We see a peppering of white birds on what might be open water or might just be more mud and reeds, but we can't get close enough to tell what they are. The birds know we're here, however, and lift off in a swooping cacophony of honks. They bank and turn in the air above us. They look bright white—snow geese, perhaps? Whatever they are, an eruption of waterfowl is a marvellous sight. They spin around the sky, cornering as precisely as a squad of dancers, and settle back down. The lake is their place, and they're not going to leave it until they decide, with their mysterious group intelligence, to continue their journey south. Later, they will bottleneck with other birds in Idaho and Nebraska to feed and rest, and then spread out again en route to their wintering grounds.

I wanted to see sandhill cranes because of a 2006 novel by Richard Powers, *The Echo Maker*. The book opens with a glorious abundance of cranes, half a million of them, who are co-present with a human disaster, in the form of a single-vehicle crash that leaves its survivor with a head injury and a rare neurological condition as a result. The condition is Capgras syndrome, in which the sufferer confabulates a belief that the people who present themselves as siblings, friends, or spouses are fakes, replicas planted to take the place of the real intimates. In Powers's book, the beauty and majesty of the cranes serve as a counterpoint to the muddles of the human characters—all of whom have, in some way, fallen short of what might have been.

For the person with Capgras, no one is who they appear to be, and the true selfhood of others is a mystery. It seems like either a metaphor or a metastasis of those uncanny but common existential fears that often beset midlife—*Am I who I could be, or should be? This person who is living my life, has it really been me all along, or have I been replaced by a more socially acceptable and docile impostor?*

Turning away from the birds, we follow a human-made trail around the outlines of the lake at its fullness. It leads through the woods to a clearing with a perfect little A-frame cabin and leaf-dusted outbuildings; a sign says we've reached the headquarters for the Beaverhill Bird Observatory's activities. I imagine an idyllic life in the A-frame, pulling electricity from the solar panels on the roof, counting and recording the visitations of birds. As a child, I dreamed about being a fire lookout on top of a mountain, self-sufficient and folded into a romanticized natural world. But the bird observatory isn't really that secluded—if we've happened on it by following the trail, there must be many others who've wandered into the clearing.

On the way back into Edmonton, we pass through the town of Tofield. It, too, is so flat as to be almost two-dimensional, but this flatness is definitely a human creation. Tofield is a small settlement—town seems too dense a word—with many near-empty lots on which repose road construction equipment and machines for farming and metal fabrication. Like most western small towns, the roads are as wide as a landing strip, lined with the usual allotment of Chinese restaurant, railway hotel with no windows on the ground floor, post office, and seniors centre. It's late Sunday afternoon, so not a time when there's much street life in such places, but in contrast to the densely occupied lake of the geese and the beavers, Tofield seems particularly still.

Recently on the CBC I heard a scientist talking about how some animal species around the world are changing their morphology—ears are getting bigger, wings are getting wider, tails are getting longer. The scientist interpreted these changes as a forced adaptation to increasing heat. Animals with greater surface area to radiate heat away from their bodies have gained a reproductive advantage in the past few decades, hence the longer-tailed shrews, the bigger-eared bats. The species in question are evolving much faster than species should evolve, it seems to me, the work of millennia compacted into a few generations. The speed of these mutations feels uncanny, but it also feels hopeful. If the shrews and bats can do what humans can't, and adapt to survival on a warming planet, they may still be here when we're gone. These are the creatures that will be accompanying me, and all the other humans, into the dying of the light.

Epilogue: Eastbound

Spring 2022, Hamilton, Ontario

IN MY SIXTH DECADE, I am westbound as a general condition, but eastbound as a traveller. Over the past two years, even as the pandemic rooted me in Edmonton, I made many trips eastward to Hamilton, where my parents lived. Flying east to Toronto, then getting the bus to Hamilton, is a form of going back in time, into my own history—as a geeky adolescent in Toronto, and even further back, beyond memory, to the generations of great-grandparents who came as settlers to the area around Guelph and St. Catharines. My history is deep here, much deeper than twenty-odd years in the west.

The first time I flew east during the pandemic was when my father experienced an abrupt decline in his health. It was the first day of October 2020, and Pearson airport was almost empty. The arrival and departure screens were blank blue oblongs. The devices for shunting crowds into planes and out to ground-side transport, the moving walk-ways and terminal trains, stood empty, waiting for a mass of travellers who never arrived. It seemed like every journey in the world had ground to a halt because of a virus. I looked out the window of the inter-terminal monorail compartment in which I was the only passenger, and the vast,

< *Fortune's spindle evergreen shrub growing in Hamilton, Ontario.* (Photo by the author.)

flat parking lots reminded me of the prairies after the crops have come in, or before the new seeds grow.

My father was in the old crowded hospital in the east end of Hamilton for a long time. In the late fall of 2020, the long time became the end, and he slipped into the twilight and over the western horizon and died. As I write this, my mother is in an assisted-living residence, making a new home in the bewilderment of new widowhood and pandemic isolation.

My brother and sister-in-law, who live about an hour away, spend many weekends going back and forth to Hamilton, helping to console my mother and ease her shock, while sorting out innumerable practical details. I'm not a regular presence, so I'm of only limited use for the tasks of organizing and sorting and running interference with doctors and social workers and bureaucrats. I do what I can on the phone—making calls, leaving messages, and hectoring overburdened health-care staff, who don't move as fast as we want them to move, to get things done for my mother. When I come to Hamilton, I spend as much time as I can with her, gauging how tired she is and how much energy she has for my visit. I book a short-stay near her residence, so I can retreat for a few hours when she's fatigued. I come and go, a visitor in the east where I used to live.

When I'm in Hamilton, everything I perceive tells me that I'm not in the west. My years in Alberta have sharpened my senses, and when I come to Ontario I notice the humidity is higher, the green tangle of leaves and vines and moss is lusher and more abundant than anything in the prairies, parklands, or badlands.

The same is true of the human abundance: in southwestern Ontario I am never quite out of the range of other people. The pulse of human activity, the hum of people living and shopping and eating and working in dense spaces, has sprawled across the region. The ruins of human habitation aren't few and far between like they are in the west; they're simply the sedimented layers of buildings and places still in use. The past is stratified and scored through by human endeavours.

Busy people are going everywhere, doing everything. But while I'm in Hamilton, I'm not busy. Hamilton these days is the place of waiting—

for visiting hours at the hospital (where both my parents were inpatients at different times), for my mother to be ready to receive visitors, for appointments with specialists in bodily and legal affairs, for the sun to set. The whole city has become, for me, a geography of waiting. I know the cafés where I can linger after I've finished my coffee, and the aimless walks I can take when I'm tired of lingering, out to the scrabbling east end and back to the genteel western neighbourhoods. When I'm here, I'm a bit directionless, passing time rather than gathering it up and forging it into a tool for getting things done, like I do at home. Mostly, I'm just waiting.

On a recent visit, my mother wanted to talk about our relatives—who they were, where they lived, who they married, and who had which children. Our family is not one of those tightly connected and intermingled clans where everyone has a vast array of cousins, great-aunts, and grandparents many generations removed, so when my mother started naming names, I paid attention. Then, during a day of waiting, I got out my laptop and began entering those names into genealogical databases.

The names started to pile up in my spreadsheet. Person after person, families, households, parents, children, spouses, a procession of births and deaths like the sun rising and setting over and over again. The sheer abundance of people available to me in southwestern Ontario contrasted with the starker, less peopled way that I experience the spaces out west.

These people, my progenitors, were Scottish (or "Scotch," as they would have said) with a sprinkling of people from northern England and a few Protestant Northern Irish, also known as Ulster-Scots. My maternal lines of descent go back to the great Scottish diaspora of the late eighteenth and early nineteenth centuries, coming from the western islands of Mull and Tiree, and the wild Marches region near the English border. They are exactly the people described by Alice Munro in her book of linked stories *The View from Castle Rock*.

They held on to their ethnic specificity for generations after they arrived in southern Ontario. When I looked up early censuses online, the Fergusons, Robinsons, McInnises, Cambells, Wilkies, McDonalds and their descendants are listed as "Scotch," even fifty, eighty, a hundred years after their ancestors arrived in Canada. Their first names are what I believe my ancestors would have considered "plain" and thus appropriate for straightforward, down-to-earth people—the men are John or William or Charles; the women are Mary or Catherine or Sarah or Jean.

The exception is my maternal grandfather, Walter Ferguson, who named his children Reginald, Wilbert, Clarence, Imogene. This makes me wonder if he and his wife were great readers of Victorian novels, or nineteenth-century poetry, or attentive to the stories from far away that filtered into their small-town Presbyterian world. Perhaps not by coincidence, this particular group of brothers and sisters contains the first person of all the generations since their arrival in Canada to attend university, and this not even a boy (which might be expected) but a girl: my grandmother Kay. (Kay's middle names were Mary Elizabeth, but her given first name was Kathleen, a variant on all the Catherines and Catrionas who preceded her.) Kay married a Methodist whose parents owned a corner store in Toronto. Her husband—my grandfather Roy—was also the first in his family to go to university, and together Kay and Roy went all the way to Sichuan, west China, as missionaries.

When I started looking for the histories of my ancestors, I was struck by how mobile they were. I had always assumed that, being settlers, they settled in a particular place, but according to old censuses, they did anything but. The geographic boundaries of their movements were narrow by the standard of the automobile, much less the airplane. Nonetheless, in an age when it would have taken several days to travel a hundred kilometres, moving that distance three times in ten years must have required a great deal of effort and willingness to move on, or perhaps it wasn't willingness so much as compulsion. There was a network of ancestors who travelled within the triangle formed by Hamilton, Kitchener, and London, and another cluster to the north, who travelled the area between Georgian Bay and Lake Simcoe. They appear to be small-town people and do not seem to have owned the land they farmed, or if they did, they sold or rented it out when they moved on.

They moved around the Indigenous lands that became known as the Haldimand Tract, the Robinson-Huron Treaty, the Williams Treaties, and the Nottawasaga Purchase. These lands, especially the southern and western parts, were stamped all over by the marks of nineteenth-century Scottish settlers, who renamed everything after places they had left behind: Caledonia, Stratford, Perth, Caithness, Lanark, Ayre, Stormont, Glengarry. It's as though they were trying to superimpose their words on the older Indigenous languages, or perhaps they had no idea that a new country—new to them—could be anything but a version of what they left behind.

Where were my ancestors going, moving all over the quasi-Scottish lands of southern Ontario? Some were itinerant labourers. Most of them could read and write, they aren't listed as boarders in the homes of other people, and, considering child mortality rates among the poorest white settlers of the time, relatively few of their children died.

My best guess, based on what my mother has told me as well as the census data, is that most were itinerant members of the very small middle class that was beginning to emerge in the late nineteenth century— never wealthy enough to build or own the sedate red-brick homes with white wood trim that still dot the small towns of southwestern Ontario, but not forced to sell their physical labour either. They were clerks, accountants, the occasional circuit-riding preacher, and many were teachers. High school teaching in those days was a mobile operation, requiring moves from one rural schoolhouse to the next.

Moving as they did, did these settlers have an attachment to the places they lived in? Did they build houses and move on within a few years, so that their old homes fell into ruins like the abandoned houses near Spaca Moskalyk? When they imagined "home," did they see the towns and villages of the borderlands of Scotland, which must have grown dimmer in memory as the years went by, or the new places, with the names they had borrowed from their grandparents' homes and superimposed on the lands of the Anishinaabe and the Huron?

My great-grandfather Walter Ferguson, the one who named his children Wilbert and Imogene, climbed the ladder of school administration to the rank of principal of the Caledonia School in the town of the same name, where he spent thirty years. He lost his wife in 1922 to "spinal sclerosis" (a degeneration of the nerves of the spine, which would probably now be diagnosed as multiple sclerosis), and one son to the Great War in the Battle of Ypres in 1915. Caledonia was the place from which his youngest child, my grandmother Kay, set forth first to university and then to China.

His own parents came from the west coast of southern Scotland, near the borderlands with England. This region is described as wild and lawless in histories of Scotland, but as far as I can tell, in the mid-nineteenth century, people were leaving for mundane and respectable reasons—no more land to be farmed, no prospects of a comfortable agricultural life for a second or third son, who would not inherit land. His wife's family came from the Hebridean islands, which were depopulated in the early nineteenth century by the collapse of the kelp-processing industry, the arrival of potato blight, and the eagerness of absentee landlords to evict tenant farmers who could no longer scrape together their rent payments from the exhausted soil.

Mr. Ferguson's letters to Kay and her husband in China are tinged with melancholy. He was well read and, by virtue of being the school principal and holder of several offices in the Presbyterian church, possibly the best-informed person in Caledonia about current events. He knew there was a wide world beyond this orbit, and that his children and their children would move into it, whereas he would not.

Writing to Kay and Roy in the 1930s, he speculates about the possibility of a "tele-vision" that would allow him to see them, and to see the grandchildren born on the other side of the world. He knows that the speed of light has been calculated, and he wonders to what use this information might be put, what wonderful technologies might displace the hard, dirty labour of the smallholder farmers around him. He sees the dire economic conditions of both Canada and Europe in the 1930s and wonders whether economic desperation will thwart the possibility of a new world order based on peace and science rather than ethnic prejudices and scarcity.

Four generations later, I'm living not only in the future he imagined, but the future beyond that. From where (and when) I sit reading his letters, in a coffee shop in Hamilton in 2022, the tele-vision is almost archaic, the nations have not come together in peace and science, and, to the best of my knowledge, none of my great-grandfather's descendants ever returned to Caledonia.

Also, the planet is on fire. Mr. Ferguson would not have been a stranger to catastrophe. The forced clearances of the Scottish Highlands would have been alive in the memories of his wife's family, his son died in the Great War when barely out of his teens, his wife died very young, and he lived through a brutal economic depression that derailed the lives of his brothers, who drifted around southwestern Ontario looking for work before they, too, died young.

But could he have imagined the climate crisis? His part of Ontario was known for apocalyptic visions during the Great Awakening revivals of charismatic Christianity in the mid-nineteenth century, but everything I know about my ancestors suggests that they would not have been caught up in this excitement, that their imaginations extended to improving the world through reason, not fantasizing about its end. What would they have made of the news of fire and ice that now pours through all information channels, and the unimaginably changed world in which their descendants will have to make their place?

If I had come across this information about my ancestors a few years ago (before I really recognized that my life was past the halfway mark)—if I had found out about the places they settled and their settler itinerancy, their persistent identification with the Scotland they left behind, their growing awareness of the big world that was neither the British Isles nor southern Ontario—it would have been interesting, as any story is inevitably interesting to the people who are part of it, even if only as genealogy. This information has a different resonance in 2022, when my own bound-in-placeness has come to occupy so much of my attention, and when I'm so conscious of the passing of time and the unknowability of what I, or we, my generation, are passing on to the ones who are taking over from us.

In Hamilton, far away from the west where I'm bound, I'm biding my time. I'm waiting as the generation before me changes into ancestors. I've been watching and attending as my parents move on ahead of me into the west, into the twilight, first my father and then my mother, joining their parents and their parents' parents. Someday, and probably not too far from now, they will both be gone, beyond the setting sun, and there will be nothing to pull me east again. Someday I'm going to make my last trip east. I will not know it is the last until it is over, until there are no more generations left between me and the western horizon.

| *My father, John Otis Kaler, born in Worcester, Massachusetts, in August 1932, died in Hamilton, Ontario, in December 2020. My mother, Hilary Kay Spooner Kaler, born in Chengdu, China, in December 1935, died in Hamilton, Ontario, in July 2022.*

Acknowledgements

I would like to express my appreciation to Michelle Lobkowicz, Mary Lou Roy, and the anonymous reviewers of the first iteration of this manuscript, for their thoughtfulness and attention to detail.

Earlier versions of "Retlaw" (Winter 2023) and "Packingtown" (Summer 2024) were published in *Queen's Quarterly*.

A portion of "Abbotsford" was published in *The Goose: A Journal of Arts, Environment, and Culture in Canada* in November 2023, under the title "Before Showtime."

Photographs by Michel Figeat are used by permission.

The photograph accompanying "Swan Hills" is licensed under the Creative Commons Attribution-ShareAlike 4.0 International License (https://creativecommons.org/licenses/by-sa/4.0/).

References

Ahlquist, D. (2014, December 2). "West of the Fifth Defined by Local Columnist." *Rimbey Review*. https://www.rimbeyreview.com/opinion/west-of-the-fifth-defined-by-local-columnist/.

Al-Akkad, O. (2019). *American War*. Random House.

Albrecht, G. (2005). *Solastalgia: A New Concept in Human Health and Identity*. PAN Partners.

Anders, C.J. (2019). *The City in the Middle of the Night*. Tor Books.

Atwood, M. (1985). *The Handmaid's Tale*. McClelland & Stewart.

Bacigulapi, P. (2015). *The Water Knife*. Knopf.

Becker, E. (1973). *The Denial of Death*. Free Press.

Bell, K. (2019, July 1). "Old Gainers Site Is a Memorial to Resistance." *Rat Creek Press*. https://ratcreek.org/old-gainers-site-is-a-memorial-to-resistance/.

Berton, P. (2001). *Klondike: The Last Great Gold Rush 1896–1899*. Random House.

Bradley, J. (2017). *Clade*. Titan Books.

Burkeman, O. (2021). *Four Thousand Weeks: Time Management for Mortals*. Allen Lane.

Butala, S. (2021). *This Strange Visible Air: Essays on Aging and Writing*. Freehand Books.

Capote, T. (1966). *In Cold Blood*. Random House.

CBC Gem. (2020, October 2). *Big Things Small Towns* (Season 2, Episode 3, St. Paul) [Video]. https://gem.cbc.ca/big-things-small-towns/s02e03.

CBC Listen. (2022, February 19). "Marking the Science and History of Timekeeping, Tick by Tick" [Radio broadcast]. In *Quirks and Quarks*. https://www.cbc.ca/listen/live-radio/1-51-quirks-and-quarks/clip/15896085-marking-science-history-timekeeping-tick-tick.

CBC Radio. (2021, September 24). "Animals Are Shapeshifting in Response to Climate Warming, and It Could Be Costing Them" [Radio broadcast]. In *Quirks and Quarks*. https://www.cbc.ca/radio/quirks/sep-25-bronze-age-town-destroyed-by-meteor-global-warming-makes-animals-shapeshift-and-more-1.6187428/animals-are-shapeshifting-in-response-to-climate-warming-and-it-could-be-costing-them-1.6187433.

CBC Radio. (2021, November 26). "George Murray Looks Back at 25 Years of Writing Poetry with *Problematica*" [Radio broadcast]. In *The Next Chapter*. https://www.cbc.ca/radio/thenextchapter/full-episode-nov-27-2021-1.6258591/george-murray-looks-back-at-25-years-of-writing-poetry-with-problematica-1.6258608. ·

Didion, J. (1968). *Slouching Towards Bethlehem: Essays*. Farrar, Straus and Giroux.

Donne, J. (2000). "Sonnet VII." In R.M. Cummings (ed.), *Seventeenth Century Poetry: An Annotated Anthology*. Wiley-Blackwell.

Fluegelman, A. (ed.). (1976). *The New Games Book*. Headlands Press.

Franzen, J. (2018). *The End of the End of the Earth: Essays*. Farrar, Straus and Giroux.

Gabbert, E. (2020). "Magnificent Desolation." In E. Gabbert, *The Unreality of Memory and Other Essays*. Farrar, Straus and Giroux.

Gawande, A. (2014). *Being Mortal: Medicine and What Matters in the End*. Metropolitan Books.

Gerson, J. (2012, August 7). "Ready and Waiting: Alberta Town Built World's First UFO Landing Pad 45 Years Ago." *National Post*. https://nationalpost.com/news/canada/ready-and-waiting-alberta-town-built-worlds-first-ufo-landing-pad-45-years-ago.

Ghosh, A. (2016, October 28). "Where Is the Fiction About Climate Change?" *The Guardian*. https://www.theguardian.com/books/2016/oct/28/amitav-ghosh-where-is-the-fiction-about-climate-change-.

Gibson, G. (2000). *Hazardous Waste, Disrupted Lives: First Nations Perspectives on the Alberta Special Waste Treatment Centre at Swan Hills*. University of Alberta Environmental Health Sciences Program.

Gilson, J. (2020). Prairie Farm Rehabilitation Administration (PFRA). In *The Canadian Encyclopedia.* https://www.thecanadianencyclopedia.ca/en/article/prairie-farm-rehabilitation-administration.

Gregoire, C. (2022). "Existential Creativity: The Role of the Artist in a Time of Crisis, in Conversation with Ruth Ozeki and Ben Okri." *Tricycle: The Buddhist Review.* Fall 2022, 52–57.

Groff, L. (2012). *Arcadia.* Voice.

Hall, J.R. (1987). *Gone from the Promised Land: Jonestown in American Cultural History.* Transaction Books.

Houriet, R. (1971). *Getting Back Together.* Coward, McCann & Geoghegan.

IPCC. (2022). *Climate Change 2022: Impacts, Adaptation and Vulnerability.* Contribution of Working Group II to the Sixth Assessment Report of the Intergovernmental Panel on Climate Change. https://www.ipcc.ch/report/ar6/wg2/.

Iyer, P. (2011). *The Global Soul: Jet Lag, Shopping Malls, and the Search for Home.* Vintage.

Jarrell, A. (2009). "Canadian Meteor Science: The First Phase." *Journal of Astronomical History and Heritage,* 12:3, 224–234.

Jones, D. (2002). *Empire of Dust: Settling and Abandoning the Prairie Dry Belt.* University of Calgary Press.

Kaplan, R.D. (1997). *The Ends of the Earth: From Togo to Turkmenistan, from Iran to Cambodia, a Journey to the Frontiers of Anarchy.* Vintage.

Kaplan, R.D. (1999). *An Empire Wilderness: Travels into America's Future.* Vintage.

Katzen, M. (1977). *Moosewood Cookbook.* Ten Speed Press.

Kingman, L. (1971). *The Peter Pan Bag.* Laurel-Leaf.

Le Guin, U.K. (1985). *Always Coming Home.* Harper & Row.

Macdonald, H. (2020). *Vesper Flights.* Random House.

Mancini, M. (2018, April 19). "15 Incredible Facts About Pigeons." *Mental Floss.* https://www.mentalfloss.com/article/535506/facts-about-pigeons.

McNichols, J. (2021, December 21). "A Ghost River Showed Its Face During the Recent Nooksack Floods." *KUOW.org* (NPR). https://www.kuow.org/stories/500-years-ago-the-nooksack-flowed-permanently-into-canada-someday-it-may-try-to-again.

Morton, T. (2013). *Hyperobjects: Philosophy and Ecology After the End of the World*. University of Minnesota Press.

Munro, A. (2006). *The View from Castle Rock*. McClelland & Stewart.

Obbard, E. (2008). *Through Julian's Window: Growing into Wholeness with Julian of Norwich*. Canterbury Press.

Orthodox Church in America. (2021). Canadian Orthodox History Project. https://orthodoxcanada.ca/Main_Page.

Peacock, N. (1996). *Life Without Water*. Longstreet.

Pocock, J. (2020). *Surrender: The Call of the American West*. Fitzcarraldo Editions.

Powers, R. (2006). *The Echo Maker*. Random House.

Powers, R. (2020). *The Overstory*. Random House.

Powers, R. (2022). *Bewilderment*. Random House.

Prairie Climate Centre. (2022). Climate Atlas of Canada. https://climateatlas.ca.

Robertson, J. (2017, November 12). "Edmonton's Cold War Command Centre Sealed Tight but not Forgotten." *CBC News*. https://www.cbc.ca/news/canada/edmonton/cold-war-atomic-nuclear-bunker-fallout-shelter-edmonton-1.4366782.

Robertson, L., Flinders, C., and Godfrey, B. (1976). *Laurel's Kitchen: A Handbook for Vegetarian Cookery and Nutrition*. Nilgiri Press.

Robinson, K.S. (1984). *The Wild Shore*. Macmillan.

Robinson, K.S. (2021). *The Ministry for the Future*. Penguin.

Scheeres, J. (2012). *A Thousand Lives: The Untold Story of Jonestown*. Free Press.

Sharratt, M. (2013). *Illuminations: A Novel of Hildegard of Bingen*. Houghton-Mifflin.

Sherrell, D. (2021). *Warmth: Coming of Age at the End of Our World*. Random House.

Solnit, R. (2006). *A Field Guide to Getting Lost*. Canongate Books.

Solnit, R. (2014). "Rattlesnake in Mailbox: Cults, Creeps, California in the 1970s." In R. Solnit, *The Encyclopedia of Trouble and Spaciousness*. Trinity University Press.

Stoltz, H. (2022, February 25). "'We Are Very Concerned': Lamont County Unable to Reach Twin Community in Ukraine."

FortSaskOnline. https://web.archive.org/web/20230727090908/ https://fortsaskonline.com/articles/we-are-very-concerned-lamont-county-unable-to-reach-twin-community-in-ukraine.

Supernant, K., Baxter, J.E., Lyons, N., and Atalay, S. (eds.). (2020). *Archaeologies of the Heart*. Springer.

Town of Swan Hills. (2022). "About Us: History." https://www.townofswanhills.com/about-us/history.

Tsing, A.L. (2015). *The Mushroom at the End of the World: On the Possibility of Life in Capitalist Ruins*. Princeton University Press.

Ukrainian Cultural Heritage Village. (n.d.). Census data for Nabyliv [*sic*]. http://www.artsrn.ualberta.ca/heritagevillage/district/villages/nebyliv.php.

Vowel, C. (2022). *Buffalo Is the New Buffalo*. Arsenal Pulp Press.

Ward, B. (trans.). (1975). *The Sayings of the Desert Fathers*. Liturgical Press.

Wells, H.G. (2002). *The Time Machine: An Invention*. Modern Library. (Original work published 1895).

Wells, L. (2021). *Believers: Making a Life at the End of the World*. Farrar, Straus and Giroux.

Wigginton, E. (ed.). (1972). *The Foxfire Book: Hog Dressing, Log Cabin Building, Mountain Crafts and Foods, Planting by the Signs, Snake Lore, Hunting Tales, Faith Healing, Moonshining, and Other Affairs of Plain Living*. Doubleday.

Wilhelm, K. (1976). *Where Late the Sweet Birds Sang*. Harper & Row.

Wray, B. (2022). *Generation Dread: Finding Purpose in an Age of Climate Crisis*. Knopf.

Wyndham, J. (1955). *The Chrysalids*. Michael Joseph.

Zwicky, J. and Bringhurst, R. (2018). *Learning to Die: Wisdom in the Age of Climate Crisis*. University of Regina Press.